HOW EFFECTIVE IS YOUR RECRUITING PROCESS?

PATRICIA KYEI KENNEDY, Ed.D

HOW EFFECTIVE IS YOUR RECRUITING PROCESS?

iUniverse books may be ordered through booksellers or by contacting:

iUniverse
1663 Liberty Drive
Bloomington, IN 47403
www.iuniverse.com
1-800-Authors (1-800-288-4677)

ISBN: 978-1-5320-7682-4 (sc)
ISBN: 978-1-5320-7683-1 (e)

Library of Congress Control Number: 2019907039

Print information available on the last page.

iUniverse rev. date: 08/18/2020

CONTENTS

DEDICATION

To my Lord and Savior Jesus Christ, who has a plan and a purpose for my life. To my father Jonathan, who encouraged me from an early age to attain higher education; and demanded that I write academically, with depth and clarity. To my husband Isaac and children (Jeremy and Jared) who have been very supportive and encouraging.

SUMMARY

With 22 years' experience in Talent Acquisition and Recruiting, plus 8 years in Human Resources, I have come to believe that companies spend more money to replace their employees instead of investing in retaining the current talent. Employers spend so much energy, time, money and other vital resources to find talent in a shrinking pool of applicants, when they can easily look at their workforce and promote from within. Most organizations continue to circle around the initial phase of Talent Management only to realize that they lose good talent to their competitors because they didn't commit to development and retention. Some of the reasons why Talent Management is not fully achieved within such organizations is the fact that there is a strong emphasis on external recruiting and less on internal promotion.

Hiring externally is great and can increase the creativity and innovation of any organization. However, that can be utilized for entry level roles, some specialized roles, and difficult to fill positions, where the right talent cannot be obtained from within the current workforce. With the practice of focusing primarily on external recruiting instead of promoting from within, leadership has increased the dissatisfaction of most employees. Current employees who are "passed over" for promotions (when they qualify for it, but an external candidate gets hired for that position) or not given a chance to interview for vacant positions conclude that they are not valued. Hence, they don't have to commit to the vision or mission of the organization, or render quality service to customers. Instead, they waste resources and even infest other team members with their low morale.

Low employee morale doesn't just develop overnight. There are many reasons why employees experience low morale at work. It can stem from issues: at home, with coworkers, management or the work itself. This book focuses on how morale, performance, intent to quit and turnover disrupts organizational revenue because of dissatisfaction with the internal recruiting or hiring practices. This book will also show how leadership and decision makers within the recruiting process have and will continue to decrease satisfaction, performance and morale and increase turnover within their organization as a result of dissatisfaction with the internal recruiting process.

The effects of low morale and performance are analyzed and the cost of these variables in addition to turnover is reviewed in depth. Turnover (whether voluntary or involuntary) in itself is good if the employee performs below par. However if the employee is a high talent or mediocre (where training can turn the performance around) – then turnover (voluntary) becomes an unnecessary hindrance to revenue.

The content of this book will help Human Resources and Talent Acquisition teams analyze their current process and determine if their process: is working; retains the right talent; decreases turnover cost. The cost of turnover is reviewed by examining total cost: per hire; for orientation; continuous training. Ample literature is reviewed and information contained will benefit leadership as they revamp their recruiting process. Results from a research conducted with employees who have participated in various recruiting and selection processes are also included in this book. Specific themes that emerged as a result of employee experiences with the recruiting process are highlighted. These themes provide information on why: dissatisfaction increases; morale, performance decreases; and turnover increases. Finally, recommendations are provided in the last chapter to provide guidance when revamping or creating a new process.

Author's note

I am a big proponent of the entire recruiting team (Talent Acquisition Specialist, hiring manager and anyone else who will be part of the decision making process) getting together and outline a plan (during the Intake Session) to review applicants (if the hiring managers want to know who is applying) and candidates after they have been interviewed. This basically means that the interviewing manager can send an email on candidates to the recruiter (or Talent Acquisition Specialist) after a candidate has been interviewed, indicating if the candidate is a YES, NO or MAYBE (including a reason for their decision). If the team works in close proximities with each other, then they can meet twice a week to discuss candidates after they have been interviewed. Every organization can choose what works best for them. However, the goal is to provide feedback immediately or in a timely manner so that the Recruitment Specialist can communicate with the candidate and create a positive experience for the candidate and the brand (organization).

CHAPTER ONE

What is wrong with your Recruiting and Hiring Process?

How effective is your recruiting process? If you are a leader or a decision maker in the recruiting process, and can answer "Yes" to all the questions below then you may not need this book. However, I will still encourage you to read it and perhaps learn new theories and strategies to recruit and retain good talent. If you answer "No" to even one of these questions, then please read the book carefully and focus on the bottom line - your: profit, market share, competitiveness and therefore: your employees, vendors and customers. By focusing on the bottom line you will be compelled to revamp your recruiting and selection process.

- Our employees believe in the Organization's mission: __YES __NO

- Our employees know where to find our job postings: __YES __NO

- Our employees apply for positions for promotions: __YES __NO

- Our employees receive immediate feedback: __YES __NO

- Our employees expect to have a positive experience: __YES __NO

- Our employees refer friends and or families to our postings: __YES __NO

- Our recruiting process gives applicants a good experience: __YES __NO

- Our recruiting process gives candidates a good experience: __YES __NO

- Our recruiting process retains talented employees: __YES __NO

Organizations exist to make money, by providing services or creating products. Every organization requires people to create or manufacture products, and or render services needed by their customers. Recruiting and selection is an integral part of the Human Resources department and entire organization. This specialized department provides services in strategic hiring for immediate and future needs. Over the years, organizations have created separate Recruiting departments that partner very closely with Human Resources. Other organizations have outsourced most or all of their recruiting efforts to a vendor known as a Recruiting Processing Outsourced (RPO). Organizations rely on efficient Talent Acquisition or Human Resources departments (with strategic recruiting partners) to meet hiring needs. Even our so called "mom and pop" shops have to adhere to some form of recruiting philosophies to hire people. Regardless of how large or small a company is, they will need to hire people. Although Talent Acquisition (uses very strategic methodology in finding the right people for the organization) and Recruitment (filling vacancies) are somehow different, for the purpose of this study, both terms will be used. Ultimately a Recruiter or a Talent Acquisition Specialist (depending on the organization) is involved in the hiring process.

Organizations are constantly competing to find, and hire the best candidates in the industry. All applicants, regardless of whether they are internal to the organization or external, have to participate in the recruiting and selection process in order to obtain growth (financial, increase in skills, knowledge, status, etc.). People participate in the recruiting and selection process in anticipation of having their intrinsic and extrinsic work values met (George & Jones, 2008). Organizational leaders recruit talented people to innovate, produce quality products, and render excellent services in order to increase profit, and maintain their competitive edge. According to Butcher and Kritsonis (2007), Human Resources Management involves recruiting, training, and retention. It's not sufficient to source and recruit the right people if leadership fails to provide training for growth and promotion. Since most people work to increase their status, lack of training will propel current employees to seek other employment outside of the firm. Potential employees can also decline to accept offers if recruiters or decision makers are unable to accurately communicate growth potentials. Thus, organizations must have a strategic and effective recruitment process, to assure external applicants and current employees that they will provide developmental opportunities. As noted by Laurent (2008), recruiting and retention is highly important to the growth, and survival of any organization.

Although recruiting and retention is critical to an organization's effectiveness, leadership continues to utilize ineffective recruiting and selection processes. This is true for all applicants: external and internal. External applicants (current contractors within the organization or people who have no relationship with the company) submit resumes or complete applications without obtaining feedback. In this age of advanced technology, it is expected that the recruiting team can respond quickly to applicants yet that doesn't happen. Almost all applicants utilize phones, iPads, computers or laptops to submit resumes and or applications very quickly. However, Sourcers and or Recruiters receive these resumes / applications in their Applicant Tracking System (ATS) fail to send feedback as to whether the resumes or applications are being considered.

Internal employees submit their applications for available jobs because they seek growth and development (McGuigan & Stamatelos, 2011); and expect to proceed through the recruitment process with hopes of obtaining a promotion or a lateral move. Regrettably, most employees do not get feedback on their applications. Some of the fortunate employees who are able to participate in the interview process may not receive feedback as to why they were not selected for promotion. If they get feedback, it might lack the information or steps that can direct them to obtain the knowledge and skills needed for future promotions.

Contractors (or temporary employees) endure a worse fate than employees because they are viewed as externals. Contractors are hired to problem solve and increase profitability. Hence if they sense a lack of value, due to negative recruiting and selection experience, productivity may decline. The absence of feedback to external applicants (especially if they are not current contractors) may not directly hamper the organization's profitability, but will have a direct correlation if internal applicants (and contractors) endure the same experience.

The lack of feedback often occurs in organizations with: flawed recruiting and selection processes; limited staff in Recruiting or Human Resources to effectively manage the process. Perkins (2011) noted that employers should give immediate feedback to candidates regarding their applications. Knowing the status of their applications or candidacy will help employees create new goals, or work towards the established goal of attaining growth opportunity. Kazi and Zadeh (2011) posit that leadership should expedite the hiring process to create a good work environment. Expediting the hiring process should afford internal employees information on their candidacy.

Regardless of what the issue is, organizations with ineffective recruiting and selection process can impede employee satisfaction, morale, performance, and increase turnover. As noted by Kazi and Zadeh (2011) leadership should recognize what their workforce values, and what satisfies them. If employees value growth and promotion, then having that opportunity will increase their satisfaction. While leadership knows the potential of their employees, they continue: to ignore some of their applications; to delay feedback after interviews; not refer them for training and development. Leadership should not fail to communicate with all internal applicants and candidates regardless of whether they meet the minimum requirement or not.

Decision makers in the recruiting process should also be mindful of their contractors because they complete tasks and meet or achieve departmental goals. Contractors help the organization to thrive by meeting Standard Levels of Agreements (SLA) and therefore require some feedback on their applications. When leaders in the hiring process fail to inform contractors or temporary employees of the status of their application or candidacy, it causes them to decrease their satisfaction. According to Aydogdu and Asikgil (2011) when employees think that there is less chances of getting promoted they get dissatisfied. Dissatisfaction ensues, because employees begin to view their intrinsic and or extrinsic values as unattainable within the department or organization.

Employee satisfaction not only influences the performance of employees, but also the performance of the organization. Mahmood, Mirza, Khan and Talib (2011) indicated that the performance of an organization is highly affected by the satisfaction of its employees. Mahmood et al. noted that the performance of employees is positively correlated with organizational performance. As employees decrease their performance, the quality of products and services decrease, and the quantity of products also decrease. A decline in employee performance can dissatisfy customers and reduce an organization's customer base. When the performances of employees are under par, customers will be dissatisfied and they will obtain products and services from the competitor. When customers are dissatisfied with products or services, organizations lose their market share, their competitive edge, and profitability.

Taking this into practicality lets view the correlation of an employee performance on an organization's performance.

A fast food worker is upset because he or she applied for a position within the restaurant and was not considered. Neither did that employee receive feedback as to why they were not hired for the role. The employee gets to work and is nonchalant about the services that they have to provide to customers. A customer orders a specific menu item but the employee returns with the wrong food item because they weren't paying attention or doesn't really care anymore. The customer refuses the food and demands the correct food item. The employee then throws the food away and has to prepare a new one for the customer. Although the customer finally receives the correct food item, they are dissatisfied with the service. The employee on the other hand doesn't care about wasting company's money (throwing out food). Time has also been wasted on both sides (employee and customer), and the customer can decide not to patronize the restaurant again. This customer can then discuss the experience with friends and family, prompting them to also stop patronizing the business. The company's brand is no longer a brand of choice.

According to George and Jones (2008) employee performance affects customer satisfaction. The correlation between employee performance and customer satisfaction is profound and crucial - so it will be mentioned numerous times in the subsequent pages.

How does an ineffective Recruiting and Selection Process influence both the employee and the organization?

Talent Acquisition Specialist / Recruiters, and hiring managers screen resumes, applications and conduct interviews to select the right candidate. Ullah (2010) noted that it is imperative for organizations to select the right candidate for the job. As a result, it behooves leadership to have a good selection process in place. Organizations task their Human Resource (those that incorporate recruiting staff) or Talent Acquisition departments to: understand the needs of the organizations; strategize; develop job descriptions; advertise job openings; source, screen and interview candidates; forward viable candidates to hiring managers; collaborate with hiring managers to make informed decisions on candidates; and consistently provide feedback to candidates on the process (McGuigan & Stamatelos, 2011).

An effective recruiting process requires sourcers and or recruiters to screen and select candidates from within or outside the organization to be interviewed. These candidates have to meet the minimum requirements of the job. When the best talents are identified, recruiters forward them to line mangers and or supervisors to continue the interview process; with the intentions of selecting the right talent for the right position. The recruiting and selection process requires immediate and continuous feedback. Recruiters / Talent Acquisition Specialist should inform candidates of decisions immediately after the interview process has been concluded. If candidates are not selected, they should be given clear and detailed feedback. Delayed feedback or the lack of it can lead to frustration, and increase employee dissatisfaction.

The frustration experienced by the candidate when feedback is delayed or never received can also be felt by the Recruiter, especially if they are waiting for the manager to make a decision. Sometimes line managers take up to a week or more to provide feedback. When hiring managers' delay in providing feedback it prompts the Recruiter to come up with excuses when contacted by the candidates. In addition, it prevents them from measuring their accomplishment for that day or that week – especially since recruitment is metrics driven. If a delay in feedback is devastating to the Recruiting Specialist, imagine how the candidate feels when they wait and don't receive feedback for weeks (sometimes it takes 2 weeks or more for applicants to get feedback on their applications, and candidates on their candidacy).

When employees are giving opportunities for growth their satisfaction increases (Asvir, Ahmad, & Bushra, 2011). However when employees feel that the organization is not helping them to achieve that growth, they become dissatisfied.

A good example is: A Call Center Representative has worked for the company for one year. She informs her manager that she has an interest in a supervisory role. Her manager knows that the Rep has the knowledge, skills and abilities, however she is lacking additional knowledge needed to be successful in the supervisory role. Her manager then suggest some training and job shadowing. When an opportunity opens up in the call center, the Rep applies for the role. The effort of the manager alone signifies that she is interested in the employee's growth. Therefore, the employee will so anything within their power to continue to increase their production so the department becomes successful. She will be friendly and helpful on the phone with customers, she will follow up with customers to resolve their inquiries. Conversely, if this same employee was ignored by her manager and wasn't provided training or challenging assignments to increase knowledge and skills, she will become unhappy and that will affect how she works. The Rep can be curt on the phone with customers, hung up the phone before inquiries are resolved, provide the wrong information to customers, etc. Dissatisfaction has a tendency to increase as: employee applications are ignored; employees are declined an opportunity to interview without feedback; and when employees are declined promotions after interviews without justifications. As dissatisfaction increases, morale and performance decrease, and the intent to leave or turnover increases. Tuzun (2007) indicated that dissatisfaction is an indication of intent to leave. As morale decreases, turnover will increase, and leadership will lose their creative employees to competitors. According to Ullah (2008), the decision making process is significant to the interviewing process, thus internal applicants and internal candidates desire to have feedback about their application or candidacy after interviews.

The ambiguity about their applications and candidacy causes internal applicants and internal candidates to become dissatisfied with the recruiting and selection process, and consequently the entire organization. There's no longer a "buy in" to organizational vision. Subsequently, dissatisfied employees decrease their morale and their attitude towards their job and work environment becomes negative. With the wrong attitude, employees might decrease their productivity and begin to think of quitting. What manager (line manager or senior manager) wants an unproductive employee? Or better yet – what manager will prefer an employee with low morale to work within their team environment. Not many, because an employee with low morale can contaminate several team members. Low morale within a team will put a strain on team problem solving and team decision making. A decrease in employee performance and an increase in turnover will cause the organization to lose its talent, decrease profitability, and affect market share. Pearce (2007) indicated that decision makers in the hiring process should provide detailed information to non-selected applicants and candidates as to why they were not selected.

Dissatisfaction with the recruiting process and the entire organization continue to escalate when non selected internal applicants and internal candidates are unable to increase their skills. Most leaders have not recognized that one of the avenues to achieve growth is through the recruiting and selection process. When leaders spend time to increase the skills of employees who have not been successful in receiving growth, satisfaction will increase. Employees will feel valued when their employer takes the time to invest in them. The lack of efforts by Human Resources, Talent Acquisition and line managers to refer such employees to the Training and Development team (for skills improvement) contributes to employee dissatisfaction.

Figures one and two illustrate the effects of an ineffective recruiting and selection process on both the employee and the organization.

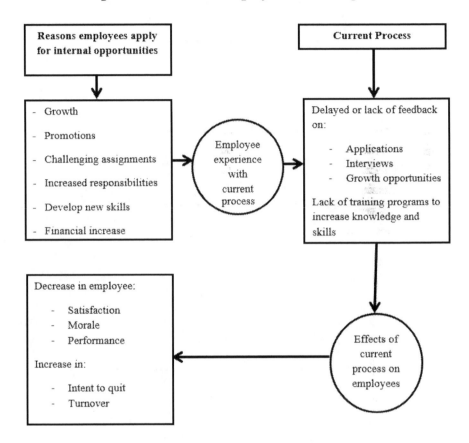

Figure 1. **Effects of an Ineffective Recruiting and Selection Process**

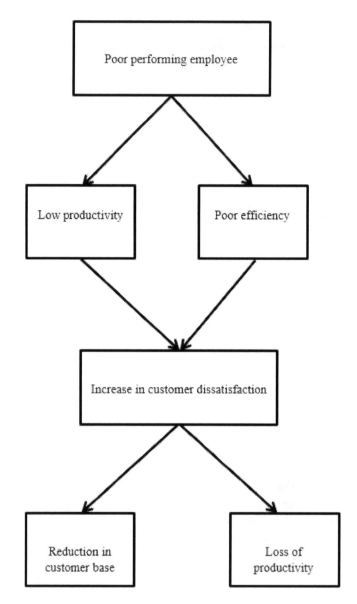

Figure 2. **Effects of an Ineffective Recruiting and Selection Process on Employee Performance and Organizational Performance**

Investing in existing employees increases satisfaction and morale, and not investing in employees propels them to leave to competitors. It's that simple. As talented employees leave the organization, there remain fewer employees with the necessary creative skills to produce and intensify organizational profitability. Leadership invests in current employees when they create opportunities for growth. When opportunities are created the hiring team should spend ample time in the selection process. Schoenherr (2009) indicated that leadership in the hiring process should invest time to find the right person and those who do not meet the minimum criteria should be informed immediately. Programs should be offered to them to enhance their skills for future opportunities.

Lack of programs for growth can lead to low morale and turnover. According to Schoenherr (2009) when leadership provides training for career development, they demonstrate that they want their employees to advance. When employees feel valued their satisfaction level increases. Schoenherr indicated that employees must feel that they are valued by their employer. As noted by George and Jones (2008) when organizations are unsuccessful in providing training and development, they are unable to retain their employees. Singer and Goodrich (2006) noted that leadership should help prepare their employees for advancement or they will leave the organization.

A decrease in morale is apparent as employees who have experienced the phenomena increases their tardiness and absenteeism, stimulating intent to leave or increased turnover. The phenomenon can be very basic: lacking knowledge on where they are in the recruiting and selection process. This simple and basic phenomenon can have a roller coaster effect. This is because a decrease in performance ensues as morale decreases and consequently affects the performance of employees and the organization. As noted by Tuzun (2007) dissatisfied employees are not retainable, therefore turnover increases with this group. Butcher and Kritsonis (2007) indicated that employees choose to leave their employer when they feel that: they are not valued; they do not have opportunities for career development and personal growth; and they are not able to develop new skills.

What is the Purpose of the Study?

To better understand the impact of recruiting on internal employees, a study was conducted with current employees within an organization. The purpose of the research was to explore the shared experiences of internal candidates who have participated in the recruiting and selection process. Specifically, the study investigated whether dissatisfaction with the recruiting and selection process decreases overall satisfaction at work. Additionally, the study examined the impact of overall satisfaction by measuring employee morale; performance; and turnover after they experience the recruiting and selection process. Morale was measured by tardiness and absenteeism, and turnover was measured by examining intent to quit.

An underlying intent of the study is to benefit to organizational leaders who want to retain their current talent, specifically high and mid performers. Retaining current talent means that leadership will: create opportunities for growth; encourage employees to apply for open positions; interview qualified internal candidates; inform non selected internal applicants or internal candidates who were not considered of reasons for rejection; and encourage non selected internal applicants, and internal candidates to attend training to increase skills and knowledge. When leadership keeps employees informed of the processes, and ensure them that they are valued, dissatisfaction will decrease. Employees will know that they are valued and they will have a good experience with the recruiting and selection process. As employees begin to feel valued, they will commit to organizational vision and goals. Such commitment will also enhance loyalty to leadership. Thus satisfaction, morale, and performance will not decrease, and consequently, tardiness, absenteeism, and turnover will decrease.

What Research Questions can be asked?

Decision makers in the recruiting and selection process have not: provided timely feedback to internal applicants and internal candidates as to why they were not selected; informed internal candidates of the necessary skills and knowledge needed in other to be selected for future positions; provided training to close skill gaps; or discussed other available positions that internal candidates might qualify for. For this reason, internal candidates have become dissatisfied with the process and the entire organization. The following research questions assisted the researcher in understanding the shared and lived experiences of employees who have experienced the phenomena. Information gained from the research questions is used to help leadership in restructuring their recruiting and selection process. Subsequently, the revamped and strategic process can increase job satisfaction, morale, performance, and decrease turnover.

Rq1 = Is there a significant difference in employee satisfaction after they experience the recruiting and selection process?

Rq2 =Is there a significant difference in employee morale (as measured by tardiness and absenteeism) after they experience the recruiting and selection process?

Rq3 = Is there a significant difference in employee performance after they experience the recruiting and selection process?

Rq4= Has intent to leave or turnover increased after employees experience the recruiting and selection process?

What Limitations and Delimitations can be found with this Study?

This study utilized interviews as the only means of data collection. Creswell (2007) noted that the primary source of data collection in a phenomenological study includes interviews, and review of documents. Limitations of the study were inherent in data collection, and were inclusive of: inability to generalize the findings to a larger population or different industries; reluctance of employees to respond to questions pertaining to intent to leave; inconsistency of interviewee responses; and the inability to review attendance records and exit interviews.

The purposeful sampling of employees from an organization within the United States increased the difficulty of generalizing the findings to other industries. Although generalizability was a limitation, several procedures was undertaken to bolster qualitative validity and qualitative reliability. According to Creswell (2009) the researcher can boost reliability during the coding process. The researcher ensured that there was consistency in the definition of codes. Throughout the coding process, data was compared with the codes to ascertain consistency. In addition, codes developed by the researcher were cross-checked with codes developed by other researchers.

Qualitative validity was achieved through various means: descriptive and interpretive validity; peer examination; cross checking information; and reflexivity. According to Maxwell (1992), descriptive and interpretive validity allows the researcher to use credible raw data, and capture the participant's perception of the experienced phenomenon. Creswell (2009) advised that the researcher's peer examine the research process. The researcher cross checked gathered data with information from literature reviews to ensure the consistency of collected data. Reflexivity increased the validity of the study, because the researcher was aware of her biases, values, and experience as a recruiter. Thus, she ensured that interpretation of data was not affected by her biases. As noted by Watts (2007), it is imperative that the researcher specifies their intentions for conducting the study.

Definition of Terms

1. **Absenteeism:** When an employee is temporary out of work.
2. **Applicant:** Anyone who expresses interest in a position by submitting a completed application, despite their qualification (OFCCP, 2010).
3. **Candidate:** Anyone who has applied for a position, meets the minimum qualification and has, or is proceeding through the interviewing process.
4. **Intent to leave:** When an individual makes a decision to leave his or her employer in the near future.
5. **Morale:** The attitude that an employee has towards his or her work environment.
6. **Satisfaction:** An employee's attitude towards the various parts of their job and the overall job that they perform (Gill, Sharma, Mathur, & Bhutani, 2012).
7. **Turnover:** An employee who permanently leaves their employer (George & Jones, 2008).

What is the Significance of Study?

Research shows that there exist a correlation between job satisfaction and turnover. There is very little research on how recruiting increases or decreases satisfaction, and how the experience impacts morale, performance, and turnover. The study will help organizational leaders recognize: that their current recruiting and selection process has, and will continue to dissatisfy employees; and hamper production and services. The study is not intended to serve as a panacea for employee dissatisfaction, low morale and production or high turnover. Instead, it should help organizational leaders: revamp their current recruiting and selection process; provide immediate and thorough feedback to non-selected applicants and candidates; and partner with the training and development team to increase the skills of identified employees for growth opportunities.

It is imperative that leadership review and revamp the current recruitment and selection practices, if they want to retain their employees to innovate and produce. Retaining talented employees equates value. Kouzes and Posner (2007) noted that when employees are valued, they create and innovate. Organizations with innovative employees increase their customer base and increase their market share.

CHAPTER TWO

What can we learn when we Review Literature?

The purpose of the study was to conduct a qualitative analysis that explored the shared experiences of internal candidates who had participated in the recruiting and selection process. The study examined employee satisfaction with the recruiting and selection process, and how it impacted: morale; performance; and turnover after they experience the phenomena. The reasons for job dissatisfaction can stem from various factors including: lack of growth opportunities (Kazi & Zadeh, 2011; McGuigan & Stamatelos, 2011; Swider, Boswell & Zimmerman, 2011); an employee's perception of not been valued by leadership (Shaikh, Bhutto & Maitlo, 2012); insufficient extrinsic rewards (White, 1995) etc.

A decrease in satisfaction does not only affect the employee's behavior, but also the organization and their customers. According to Tracey and Hinkin (2008) using ineffective recruiting efforts increases turnover, and the cost of turnover is due to poor job fit and organization fit. Ample literature was reviewed to understand the causes of job dissatisfaction, and what leadership needs to do to increase employee satisfaction. For the purpose of this research, emphasis was placed on literature that highlights dissatisfaction and satisfaction associated with the job within the organization, and not outside of the organization

Specific literature on the effects of recruiting on employee satisfaction, morale, performance, and turnover is lacking. Westover, Westover and Westover (2010) posit that absenteeism, performance and turnover are correlated to job satisfaction. However there is no research that links, a decrease in morale, an increase in performance, and an increase in turnover to an employee's dissatisfaction with the recruiting and selection process. There is limited relevant literature on how morale increases turnover, and the correlation between performance and morale. Nonetheless, there is sufficient and relevant literature on: satisfaction and promotion; satisfaction and performance; satisfaction and morale; and satisfaction and turnover.

Going back to the Call Center example: The dissatisfied Rep continues to be curt on the phone with customers and her "time to handle calls" is much shorter than the "average call handle time". Instead of 3 to 5 minutes on each call she is spending less than a minute on calls. She has also decided to call out sick once a week – because she is using all her sick days to interview for new opportunities with a competitor.

Most of the literature on the above variables are current, and were conducted from a quantitative perspective. As some research identifies a strong correlation among some of the variables, other research conclusively shows a moderate or even a weak correlation amongst satisfaction, morale, performance and turnover. Available research on the correlation amongst variables: satisfaction; morale; performance; and turnover will help bolster the study on how these variables can be impacted by dissatisfaction with an ineffective recruiting process. To increase performance of the organization, leadership must ensure that employees are satisfied.

Satisfaction

Satisfaction is defined as an employee's attitude towards the various parts of their job and the overall job that they perform (Gill, Sharma, Mathur, & Bhutani, 2012). Therefore, an employee's attitude towards their coworkers and managers can also affect their satisfaction. Satisfaction can be high or very low, and can change depending on met needs or experiences which influence an employee's feelings or beliefs (George & Jones, 2008). Since employees' experience in the workplace influences their satisfaction at work; satisfaction is not permanent. Satisfaction can be derived through intrinsic or extrinsic motivation. According to Daft (2008) motivation is inherent in satisfaction, because it can lead to behaviors that reflect high performance within the organization. Satisfaction can be achieved extrinsically when employees receive: salary increases; good medical coverage; good working conditions, etc. According to Herzberg (2003) employees are more satisfied when they receive motivators, which he identified as intrinsic rewards. Herzberg indicated that motivators are:

growth opportunities; job enrichment; challenging opportunities; work reorganization, etc. Herzberg concluded that these motivators are higher needs; they are lasting and increases employee performance.

Research by Mahmood et al. (2011) showed that all of Herzberg's motivator's significantly influenced job satisfaction. The research revealed that when employees obtain growth, recognition, additional responsibilities, etc., their satisfaction towards their job will increase. When employees are able to work on challenging assignments consistently it reduces voluntary turnover (Preenen, De Pater, Van Vianen & Laura Keijzer, 2011), and might serve as a means to retain employees (Podsakoff, LePine & LePine, 2007). George and Jones (2008) noted that when employees are intrinsically motivated, they use creative means to problem solve, and creativity propels organizations for success (Kouzes & Posner, 2007).

Let's take a look at a Teller within a bank. The teller has been working at the bank for two years. He is responsible for counting the drawer, cashing checks, handling deposits and selling credits cards. In addition the Teller refers members to the Financial Center Representative (for mortgages and CD's) and the Investment Advisor (for investment needs). The Teller has an insatiable appetite to grow and informs the Branch Manager during their One-on One of his desire to become an Advisor. The branch manager provides information on how the Teller can obtain his Series 6, 7, 63, 65 or 66. The bank provides the materials for the Teller to study and hopefully pass the FINRA (Financial Industry Regulatory Authority) Exams. The Teller is also allowed to "shadow" some of the Advisors at the branch. The Branch Manager's efforts reveals that the Teller is valued. The Teller in turn continues to excel because he sees "a light at the end of the tunnel". He is motivated because he is preparing for additional responsibilities. The Teller believes that once there is an opening, he will be able to interview for an Advisory job with his acquired licenses and newly developed skills.

Organizational success is influenced by customer satisfaction, thus developed employees feel valued, perform better and render the best services to customers (Goldsmith, Greenberg, Robertson & Hu-Chan, 2003). Rehman and Waheed (2011) postulate that leadership examine the nature of the employee's job in order to understand what triggers employee satisfaction. Leadership should focus on: what the job entails; the motivation of the employee to continuously perform the same task over and over again; whether the employee is acquiring new skills and knowledge as they perform the task, etc.

Employees with a positive attitude towards their job are more satisfied than employees with a negative attitude towards their job. According to Shaikh et al. (2012) dissatisfaction occurs when employees experience factors such as lack of opportunities, feeling undervalued, low salaries, etc. There exists consistent research on how satisfaction can be achieved in the work place. Research on satisfaction and promotion can help leadership create opportunities for employees, and demonstrate that they value their knowledge skills and abilities. In addition, providing growth opportunities can act as a panacea to retain talented employees.

Satisfaction and Promotion

The relationship between satisfaction and promotion has been researched for several decades, and consistently shows that there is a strong positive correlation between the two variables. Herzberg (2003) noted that satisfaction is achieved when growth and advancement are obtained. According to George and Jones (2008) when employees are denied a promotion or a job transfer, their satisfaction can be affected.

We can recall the example of the Call Center Representative – who was not promoted and experienced a decrease in satisfaction and consequently decreased performance and increased tardiness. Consequently she shows up to work one day and gives her manager her resignation letter, takes her personal items off her desk and walks out. She doesn't give the HR department an opportunity to participate in an Exit Interview - which can help leadership understand the dissatisfaction and turnover. Her immediate voluntary turnover causes the department to shuffle to find immediate solutions to meet customer needs. This also "puts" an additional stress on the current team because some will have to work long hours and handle additional calls to customer needs.

Dissatisfaction causes employees to perform under par, and they add little to organizational achievements. According to Aydogdu and Asikgil (2011) when employees think that there are less chances of getting promoted, they get dissatisfied. Employees seek advancement and growth (McGuigan & Stamatelos, 2011), and when there are no promotional or lateral opportunities dissatisfaction is ultimately the end result. Conversely, when opportunities are available for employees to increase their skills, problem solve, make decisions and add value, their satisfaction level will increase. Rehman and Waheed (2011) stated that when leadership affords employees growth, they become satisfied, and their satisfaction influences their commitment to the organization, their performance and retention.

Employees desire growth and when that is provided, they increase their satisfaction. Kazi and Zadeh (2011) indicated that when an employee lacks opportunity for growth or advancement it can increase their desire to leave the organization, because growth opportunities increase satisfaction. Organizations that fail to provide skill enhancement or developmental opportunities can increase employee dissatisfaction. Developmental programs prepare employees for internal opportunities (Trevor & Nyberg, 2008) that challenges employees and increases satisfaction.

When employees are promoted they enhance their skills through challenging assignments. These challenging assignments leads to on-the-job learning and development (Preenen et al, 2011), and increases satisfaction. Challenging job assignments also helps leadership evaluate an employee's promotability. Employees who perform challenging tasks are prepared and able to perform at higher job levels than employees who perform non challenging tasks (De Pater, Van Vianen, Bechtoldt & Klehe, 2009).

Referring back to the Teller at the bank - he received an opportunity to "shadow" Financial Advisors at the branch. He is now interfacing with "high net worth" customers and is acquiring additional skills and knowledge to be successful. Besides the bank provided the materials that he needed to study and pass the FINRA exams. With such an investment in the Teller's career, his satisfaction will increase, he will be amicable, have a wiliness to go to work early, stay late and meet expectations. Eventually a Financial Advisor position is created (Addition to Staff) because the bank experiences an increase in customers who have investment needs. The Teller applies for the position (now that he has passed the FINRA exams), he is interviewed along with other candidates and he is offered the position to become a Financial Advisor. After the promotion, he works diligently, offers outstanding services to his clients and increases his book of business. This ultimately improves the revenue and profitability of the branch / bank.

Promotions confirm to employees that they are valued and are being rewarded for exceptional performance. According to Asvir et al. (2011) employees are satisfied when leadership recognizes their value and provides them with promotions. Promotions allow employees to be challenged with additional responsibilities and become productive, thus increasing the sustainability of organizational competitiveness. Asvir et al. conducted a quantitative analysis and sampled 1500 employees from 4 glass companies in Pakistan. Regression analysis showed R value as .430, and the value of t = 5.919, P<.05 (p. 304). R value revealed a moderate relationship between internal promotion and job satisfaction and the t value revealed that the relationship between the two variables were highly significant at .000. Asvir et al. noted that promotion predicts satisfaction.

Promotion is a predictor of satisfaction, because when employees obtain growth opportunities, they will be satisfied. It is necessary for leaders to promote talented employees, because it increases challenging assignments and employee salaries. Leadership should also provide training for employees who seek advancement so that they can develop the necessary skills needed to be successful. Providing training and promotions signifies that: employees are valued; and leadership desires to invest in them. Murray and Fischer (2010) noted that organizations should hire and promote candidates who are qualified and share in the organization's value and vision. When employees share the visions and values of the organization, it becomes easy for leadership to obtain a buy in (Kouzes & Posner, 2007).

Satisfaction and Morale

Morale is the attitude that an employee has towards their work environment. Research on morale and satisfaction is debatable. As some studies denote a positive correlation between morale and satisfaction, others note that there is a weak relationship. Regardless of how strong or weak the relationship, research shows that satisfaction does influence morale at work. According to Kazi and Zadeh (2011) employees with high job satisfaction will have positive attitudes which will result in increased performance. When employees increase performance, they render quality service and productivity.

Let's take a look at a Registered Nurse at a local hospital. The Nurse is working at Triage in the Emergency Room (ER) and is the "first point of contact". When patients go to the Triage area, the Nurse: makes an assessment; places them in a room or the waiting area; and informs them of what they can anticipate (i.e., CT scan, blood work, IV, etc.). By telling them what to anticipate, the Nurse is able to "calm down" the patient and or family, and reduces unnecessary anxieties. She attends to people who walk to the ER waiting area with great care and efficiency. This nurse has a good attitude and aids in comforting patients and families. The Nurse is satisfied in her current role and has a great attitude, when managerial opportunities are available she may apply or may not because she is satisfied in her current role.

Tuzun (2007) stated that an employee's attitude towards their job will be positive if their satisfaction level is high. Cho and Perry (2011) noted that intrinsic motivation has a direct influence on employees attitudes, thus it causes change by increasing performance.

For decades studies have attempted to identify the causes of absenteeism and how to reduce it. There are several reasons why employees are absent from work, and job dissatisfaction can be a factor. Absenteeism occurs when an employee is out of work, and it is prevalent within every organization. Thus, when employees are dissatisfied at work, tardiness will increase and the propensity to call out of work will increase. Aydogdu and Asikgil (2011) noted that absenteeism is related to job dissatisfaction; however George and Jones (2008) indicated that there is a weak correlation between absenteeism and satisfaction.

Let's review the same Triage Nurse in the Emergency room. This time she is dissatisfied in her role and the department and she applies for a managerial role. The Nurse is interviewed, however she doesn't get the position, and is not told why she wasn't selected. The interviewers conclude that she lacks customer service skills and is not team oriented, and can't be a manager. Within a week she calls out sick, 30 minutes before her start time (instead of calling 2 hours earlier). This behavior continuous for a month where she calls out once a week. And she doesn't care that she hasn't given her manager ample notice to call other nurses to cover her shift. The other nurses who work with her are given additional cases because of her absenteeism. Morale of these nurses have decreased and there's constant bickering amongst the ER Nurses because of the additional work and long hours. Patients have to now wait longer before they are attended to. Most patients walk out of the ER and go to an Urgent Care to be seen. Patient surveys about their hospital visit becomes negative and decide that this specific hospital is not a hospital of choice. The negativity that stemmed from a dissatisfied nurse with low morale has now affected the nursing staff in the ER, patients and the entire hospital.

While George and Jones (2008) noted a weak correlation between absenteeism and satisfaction, they posit that satisfied employees do sometimes miss work. Granted that satisfied employees have low absentee rates, they sometimes miss work due to circumstances beyond their control, such as illness. Although Ybema, Smulders and Bongers (2010) indicated that absenteeism is not positively correlated to job satisfaction, they noted that an increase in absenteeism increases job dissatisfaction. The more an employee chooses not to go to work on their regularly scheduled days, the more dissatisfied they will be with their work. Ybema et al. postulated that absenteeism affects productivity. When employees are out of work, the quantity of production and quality of services decreases because there are limited people to render services to customers (Hausknecht et al., 2009). As a result of low productivity and poor quality, customer satisfaction decreases.

George and Jones indicated that absenteeism is costly to organizations and Kuzmits and Adam (2009) concluded that US organizations experience a serious threat due to employee absenteeism because it affects productivity, and the organization. According to George and Jones, the cost of absenteeism to US companies is approximately $40 billion. Mukherjee (2011) noted that to boost employee morale, leadership should continually provide opportunities where employees can increase their roles and responsibilities. Mukherjee concluded that if leadership provides growth opportunities to employees, the organization will also be successful.

Satisfaction and Performance

The influence of employee satisfaction on employee performance has shown not to be strong. Westover et al. (2010) noted that there is a moderate correlation between performance and satisfaction. George and Jones (2008) indicated that there exists a weak correlation between performance and job satisfaction. Research by Aydogdu and Asikgil (2011) revealed a weak correlation between job satisfaction and performance. An employee will not perform less when they experience dissatisfaction with their job, or with variables associated with their job. As a result, satisfaction is not a predictor of employee performance.

Shaikh et al. (2012) conducted a study with bank employees to determine the relationship between job satisfaction and performance. The results showed that satisfaction is not a strong predictor of job performance. Although most of the research on satisfaction and performance has shown a weak or moderate relationship between the variables, research by Rehman & Waheed (2011) showed otherwise. Rehman and Waheed calculated correlation coefficients to describe the relationship between job satisfaction and performance, and found that the relationship was highly significant at 0.52. Lloyd (2012) postulated that leadership can motivate employees to increase their performance by providing them with challenging assignments. George and Jones (2008) noted that when employees understand the correlation between performance and promotion, they get motivated to increase their performance.

Although employee satisfaction is not a precursor to employee performance, employee performance dictates organizational performance. Research has linked employee performance to organizational performance and customer satisfaction. George and Jones noted that employee performance affects customer satisfaction. When employees produce quality products and services, it increases organizational performance and market share. Conversely, when employees decrease their performance customer dissatisfaction will increase (Hausknecht, Trevor & Howard, 2009). Mahmood et al. (2011) indicated that employee satisfaction highly affects the performance of the organization. To increase the performance of the organization, Asvir et al. (2011) suggested that leadership commit to their employees. Committing to employees requires leadership to know what employees value, and make all possible efforts to meet those needs.

Turnover

Though absenteeism is temporary, turnover is permanent. Turnover occurs when an employee permanently leaves their employer (George & Jones, 2008). Turnover is very important to Human Resources Management because organizations spend significant amount of money and time to recruit, train and develop employees only to lose them to other firms.

Weller, Holtom, Matiaske and Mellewigt (2009) noted that most turnovers occur in the first two years of the employee's tenure. Employee turnover is a never ending problem and very costly to organizations (Rehman & Waheed, 2011; Yang, Wan & Fu, 2012). There are two types of turnover: voluntary and involuntary; and there are costs associated irrespective of the type of turnover. Cho, Johanson and Guchait (2009) noted that there is an influence of voluntary and involuntary turnover on recruitment and training cost, as Human Resources continuously hire and train new employees to replace terminated employees.

Voluntary turnover ensues when an employee decides to leave their employment, thus the employee has autonomy with this decision. As noted by Kazi and Zadeh (2011) voluntary turnover often occurs when an employee is dissatisfied with the job itself. Hom, Roberson and Ellis (2008) noted that voluntary turnover increases during the first year and steadily declines after that. *A good example can be seen when a company decides to hire 30 people for their Call Center. The new hires pass the background check and are put through 6 weeks of training. During training some of the new hires decide that they don't like the stressful environment so they resign. After training, a couple of new hires find out that competitor is paying $0.50 an hour more than they earn, so they also resign.*

According to White (1995), voluntary turnover results when there are: defective hiring practices; and low compensation structures. Employees can voluntarily leave a department and join another department, leading to internal turnover. However, the exit of employees to other organizations is considered external turnover and is associated with high costs. Voluntary turnover is preceded by an employee's intent to leave. Intent to leave is when an individual makes a decision to leave his or her employer in the near future. In contrast, involuntary turnover occurs when the employer terminates the employment of the employee. Employers can terminate employees through downsizing and reduce their headcount to a target level (Trevor & Nyberg, 2008).

Turnover and Performance

Employee performance, like satisfaction affects the success and sustainability of any organization. Organizations depend on their manpower to produce quality products and render quality services to their customers so as to increase their profitability. George and Jones (2008) postulated that customer satisfaction is contingent on employee performance. Thus, when employees render quality service and produce quality products, the organization acquire a large customer base, increase market share, and strengthen their competitive edge. As organizations lose their high performers or even mediocre employees, leadership has fewer people to rely on to satisfy their customers. Employee turnover affects customer service and negatively impacts the organization's revenue and profitability, specifically in the hospitality industry (Tracey & Hinkin, 2008). For this reason, performance and turnover are major concerns for Human Resources.

Hausknecht et al. (2009) noted that when organizations lose its employees, the quality of services rendered to customers decrease. Hausknecht et al. conducted a study to determine the impact of voluntary turnover on customer service quality. They sampled 5,631 employees with 88.9% response rate, and 59,602 customers with 27.6% response rate from a large leisure and hospitality organization (p. 1070). Results revealed that as voluntary turnover increased by 1-standard deviation, there was a correspondent decrease in customer service quality perceptions of .029 (p.1072). According to Hausknecht et al., the statistical significance in the relationship might be due to the lack of staff, and the time spent to train new employees instead of investing in producing quality products and services.

Consistent with the findings by Hausknecht et al. are the results from a study by Kacmar, Andrews, Van Rooy, Steilberg, and Cerrone (2006). Kacmar et al. sampled 262 out of 583 corporately owned Burger King Restaurants in the United States. Data was collected for 2 years, from 2001 to 2002, to determine the effects of managerial and crew turnover on efficiency, sales, and profits. Efficiency was measured as customer wait time, and the average food that was wasted for 2001 fiscal year (p. 137). Results revealed that: crew member turnover influenced efficiency; and managerial turnover increased crew member turnover.

As managers resigned or quit from the restaurants, turnover increased amongst crew members who were loyal and committed to the manager. When turnover increased with crew members efficiency decreased, because there were fewer remaining seasoned employees to meet customer needs. Profits decreased due to mistakes made by new hires when they served customers with wrong orders, and when food was thrown out instead of sold. Kacmar et al. concluded that turnover has an immediate influence on efficiency and profits, because of the limited staff available to service customers and the time needed to appropriately train new staff.

Ample time is needed to train new employees for them to acquire the knowledge and skills needed to perform (Tracey & Hinkin, 2008). Kacmar (2006) noted that in spite of the fact that new employees have to learn new task and increase efficiency, they are apt to make mistakes. Therefore it is necessary for moderately or highly satisfied employees to increase their performance and render quality services to customers. Edwards, Bell, Arthur and Decuir (2008) noted that satisfied employees will exhibit contextual behaviors, volunteer their time and ask for extra work. Less satisfied employees will not perform additional duties when customer satisfaction is low. As noted by Pare and Tremblay (2006), when employees are unwilling to exhibit contextual behaviors they might have intentions of quitting.

The relationship between job performance and voluntary turnover can be mediated by job satisfaction (Nyberg, 2010). Nyberg researched the relationship between job performance, satisfaction and voluntary turnover as it relates to the retention of high performance. He sampled 12,545 employees within a large insurance industry in the United States from 2001 to 2006. Nyberg measured: performance; voluntary turnover; satisfaction; promotion rate and other variables. Results showed that the coefficient for job performance was statistically significant at $p < .001$ and changed from -.18 to -.15 when job satisfaction was included. The results revealed that the relationship between performance and turnover is mediated by job satisfaction.

Zimmerman and Darnold (2007) noted that job performance influences voluntary turnover directly, and indirectly influences intent to quit. Although the relationship between performance and intent to quit, and turnover varies, data shows that there is an influence. How employees perform at work determines whether they have intentions of quitting or not. Employees who have intentions of leaving do not perform up to par (Tracey & Hinkin, 2008). When employees decrease their performance because of job dissatisfaction, it is likely that they have made a conscious decision to quit their employment.

The conscious decision to quit might be due to an experienced dissatisfaction with the job or organization. Zimmerman and Darnold (2007) used meta-analysis to calculate the true score estimates of the relationship between performance and intent to quit; and between performance and turnover. The sample size consisted of sales and healthcare professionals who had college degrees. Results showed a direct relationship between performance and turnover at -0.10; and an indirect relationship between performance and turnover at -0.18 (p. 153).

Turnover, Intent to leave and Satisfaction

Just as employee performance is inherent to the success of organizations, so is the satisfaction that employees derive from their jobs and variables that affect their job. The study on turnover and satisfaction has yielded consistent support for the relationship amongst the variables. Some research proposes that there is a strong correlation between the variables and other research suggest a moderate relationship. According to George and Jones (2008), a decrease in job satisfaction can boost intent to leave and subsequently turnover will follow. Kazi and Zadeh (2011) posit a correlation between job satisfaction and employee turnover. Although studies show a consistent relationship between job satisfaction and turnover, Mobley (1977) noted that the relationship is not strong because it is not a direct relationship.

Mobley developed a traditional turnover model that suggests mediating factors between job satisfaction and turnover. Mobley's model outlines the psychological and perceptual process that employees experience when they are dissatisfied with the job or other factors that affects the job. Mobley's model posits that employees: evaluate their current job; become dissatisfied or satisfaction decreases; think of quitting; evaluate the cost of quitting; search for alternatives; evaluate alternative; compare alternatives to present job; and make decisions to quit or stay. Mobley's model expresses what occurs when employees apply for positions within their organizations and experience dissatisfaction with the recruiting and selection process. While the model illustrates an indirect relationship between satisfaction and turnover, it does propose that job dissatisfaction causes the employee to think about quitting.

When the experience with the recruiting and selection process is unpleasant, employees realize that they are undervalued and have no future within the department or organization. Thus, employees start thinking about quitting and begin to decrease their performance. They begin to evaluate the cost of quitting which might mean: quit and stay at home; or the cost of a job search including traveling for interviews. Employees then search for alternatives within the organization, or outside the organization. They evaluate alternatives and ascertain if the alternatives are better than their current job or situation. Employees determine if the new job, department and or organization will be better than their current situation. Depending on the evaluation, employees might choose to: stay in their position; remain with the current organization and continue to apply for future opportunities; intent to quit; or quit.

Allen, Renn, Moffitt and Vardaman (2007) noted that quitting a job is associated with risks. Hence, some employees might choose not to quit even though they are dissatisfied, because the risk involved might be too great. Such employees will remain in their current position and perform below par, not adding any value to the success of the organization. Hence, they become a liability to the organization. Although Mobley's model depicts what happens when employees experience the phenomenon, there are some employees who will choose not to go through the process of evaluating alternative. Instead, such employees quit immediately they experience dissatisfaction with the recruiting and selection process. Employees who quit immediately may place more emphasis on the experienced dissatisfaction, rather than evaluating alternatives and the risk associated with quitting.

Swider et al. (2011) indicated that when employees are less satisfied at work and have alternatives, they will search for other jobs. Thus, they are more likely to leave their current organization. Such employees will not necessarily be searching for jobs within only the organization, but also outside of the organization with other competitors. There are yet other employees who may be moderately satisfied and not search for alternatives. These employees will quit only after they receive unsolicited job offers (Lee, Gerhart, Weller, and Trevor, 2008). Lee et al. sampled 14,360 people to understand the importance of unsolicited job offers in voluntary turnover. There were 6,198 respondents and 23% of them quit their jobs because of unsolicited job offers (p. 665). They noted that unsolicited job offers can trigger relatively satisfied employees to voluntarily terminate their employment with their employers.

Aydogdu and Asikgil (2011) noted that job satisfaction affects an employee's decision to stay or leave the organization, because a decrease in job satisfaction will lead to an increase in intent to leave. Studies that have linked satisfaction and turnover have revealed that some turnover is good. When an employee sub performs, then voluntary turnover is good (Weller, Holtom, Matiaske & Mellewigt, 2009). Voluntary turnover amongst poor performers can be beneficial to the organization, because some of these employees may not be desirable to retain. Conversely, voluntary turnover amongst high performers can hurt the organization. Research has suggested strategies to curb turnover due to dissatisfaction amongst talented and valued employees. As noted by Aydogdu and Asikgil leadership should reduce turnover of talented employees. Rehman and Waheed (2011) conducted research on the relationship between job satisfaction and job retention, and found that the relationship was highly significant with r = 0.34 (p. 175). They noted that an employee's satisfaction at work influenced the employee's commitment to the organization and employee retention.

When employees are happy with their jobs, they will increase their commitment to the organizational vision and commit to helping the organization achieve its goals. Helping the organization attain its goals requires employees to: remain within the organization; commit to the organization's vision; and align their values with that of the organization. Kazi and Zadeh (2011) noted that employees will quit when they are not committed to achieving organizational goals. Pare and Tremblay (2007) posit that employees with strong affective commitment or strong attachment to the organization are easily retainable, because they want to remain within the organization. Kouzes and Posner (2007) noted that employees are more committed when they share in the organizations vision, thus increasing retention. According to Harman, Lee, Mitchell, Felps and Owens (2007) the personal values and career goals of employees must be compatible with the organization. Asvir et al. (2011) indicated that organizations must put in a lot of effort to retain their employees and reduce turnover. Research by Kazi and Zadeh (2011) suggested that Human Resources can help to reduce voluntary turnover by recognizing factors that lead to turnover and taking strategic steps to reduce it.

To ensure that leadership retains their high performers, Swider et al. (2011) proposed that leadership create growth opportunities, job enrichment, development, etc. to increase job embeddedness and reduce job searches. Shaw, Dineen, Fang and Vellella (2009) indicated that when Human Resources Management inducements and investments such as career enhancements are high, voluntary turnover decreases. Harman et al. (2007) posits that the job embeddedness should link employees to other people and activities within the organization, making it difficult for employees to break those links. The higher the job embeddedness, the more satisfaction will increase, and the less likely turnover will occur.

As employees develop strong relationships, get involved in projects (Weller et al. 2009), problem solve and make decisions (George & Jones, 2008), they begin to feel that they are valuable members of the organization, making it difficult for them to quit. Leadership can empower employees to perform a variety of roles and responsibilities so as to increase employee influence (Pare & Tremblay, 2007). When employees have influence they are quick to problem solve. Preenen et al. (2011) noted that challenging assignments reduces job search behavior and intentions to leave. Their study examined the results of using challenging assignments to reduce: turnover intentions; job search behaviors and voluntary turnover. A two-wave panel study that measured behavior of 702 employees in the healthcare and welfare industries in the Netherlands was utilized. Challenging assignments, learning acquired on the job, turnover intentions, job search behaviors at Time 1; and the actual turnover that occurred after 2 years was measured at Time 2 (p. 316).

Results of the study by Preenen et al. (2011) revealed that respondents who received challenging assignments from their supervisors increased learning on the job, and consequently job searches and turnover intentions decreased. Respondents who had high turnover intentions at Time 1 reduced job search behaviors when they received continuous challenging job assignments. However, some of the respondents who had low turnover intentions at Time 1 left their organizations at Time 2 because of a decrease in challenging assignments. The findings indicated that dissatisfied employees can increase their satisfaction when giving challenging assignments to increase on-the-job learning. At the same time, satisfied employees can experience dissatisfaction when there is a decrease in challenging assignments, and continuous learning is stifled.

To retain employees and reduce turnover, leadership must recognize the needs and values of their employees, and create environments that fosters growth and creativity (Kouzes & Posner, 2007), thus increasing employee loyalty and commitment to the organization. Yang et al. (2010) conducted a qualitative study on turnover and retention strategies, and noticed that turnover is caused by unmet employee expectations. They suggested that leadership motivate employees extrinsically and intrinsically, to increase: employee satisfaction; organization commitment; and decrease turnover. Tuzun (2007), and Huning and Thompson (2001) indicated that job satisfaction predicts intent to leave because if employees are not satisfied, they will begin to make decisions to leave their employer in the near future. Voluntary turnover will ultimately be the result, if dissatisfaction continuous.

Turnover Cost

Organizations invest a lot of money to recruit, train and develop employees, in addition to offering compensation packages and other benefits. As employee turnover increases, the cost to the organization also increases (Kazi & Zadeh, 2011; Tracey & Hinkin, 2008). For this reason, organizations place high emphasis on Human Resources Management and practices to curtail turnover intentions and turnover. The cost of turnover is so astronomical that it impairs organizational revenue. White (1995) indicated that fast food, retail, healthcare, trucking, and convenient store industries have turnover rates that exceed 75%. According to Rehman and Waheed (2011), the cost of voluntary and involuntary turnover to American industries is approximately $11 billion annually. Kacmar et al. (2006) noted that it cost the food industry $4.3 billion a year to train new staff as a result of turnover.

To reduce loss of employees and associated cost to the organization, leadership must understand and address factors that increase intentions to quit and turnover. As leadership begins to understand the causes of turnover, they will put best practices in place to reduce turnover (Kacmar et al. 2006), retain their employees, and help their organizations stay competitive (Preenen et al., 2011). Tracey and Hinkin (2008) distinguished between three types of costs that affect turnover directly and indirectly: hard costs; soft costs and opportunity costs. Hard costs are tangible expenses associated with advertisements (Tracey & Hinkin). Hard costs are easily measured and quantified, because they are costs that are paid out to vendors for services, and to employees for referrals.

Human Resources must advertise during the recruitment process to increase their applicant pool. Advertising positions can be done through various mediums: internet; radio; television; newspapers, job fairs, etc. According to Tracey and Hinkin, Human Resources can calculate the cost spent on each new hire by: dividing the annual total expenses expenditure by the number of applicants. If the annual total expenses for recruiting call center associates is $100,000, and 150 applicants applied for positions for 20 positions, then the calculation is: $100,000 / 150 = $666.66. That means the organization spent $666.66 to attract each applicant.

In addition to the cost associated with recruitment, the organization incurs cost during the selection process. Tracey and Hinkin (2008) noted that this phase includes hard and soft costs. Human Resources invest hours screening resumes to identify viable candidates who meet the minimum qualification for the position. After candidates have been identified, time is spent during the interviewing process to ascertain the right candidate for the job and organization. Depending on the positions, assessments through various testing are included in this process. The time spent on applicants and corresponding paperwork during the selection process are soft costs. Testing packages and tools are tangible cost that the organization pays to a vendor.

According to Tracey and Hinkin (2008), soft cost can be calculated by multiplying the hourly wage of staff by the time spent on tasks. If 3 people are involved in the selection process with hourly wages of $15, $20, $30 respectively, and each person invests a total of 4 hours on identifying 1 candidate, then the total soft cost will be: $15 + $20 + $30 x 4 = $260. White (1995) indicated that cost associated with the selection process is detrimental to the profitability of larger organizations. Large organizations with high turnovers require more staff to participate in the selection process, and the higher the turnover, the higher the cost. Aside from the soft cost associated with the selection process, the organization incurs hard and direct cost, as Human Resources partners with various vendors to conduct the background checks of identified candidates.

After employees are hired, they go through an orientation process during their first week or first month of employment. The orientation process requires Human Resources to review policies, procedures and benefit plans. Sometimes, Human Resources partners with a vendor from an insurance company to facilitate the Explanation of Benefits section / phase. After employees are on-boarded, they receive on-the-job training from peers and or supervisors. Some of the training can be held at other locations that require traveling, lodging and meals. Additionally, various trainings via web are provided during employees' tenure to increase their knowledge.

The cost associated with the orientation process and training is both hard and soft costs. According to Tracey and Hinkin (2008) organizations can estimate the soft costs by multiplying the hourly wage of staff by the time spent on facilitating orientations. In addition, the cost of training new hires can be estimated when the hourly wages of peers are multiplied by the hours spent in training. If an Accounts Receivable Clerk earns an hourly rate of $17 per hour, and uses two weeks to train a new clerk (for the same role) then the total cost will be: $17 x 80 (8 hours a day x 10 business days) = $1,360. Weller et al. (2009) noted that the cost of investment in training and development is lower when turnover occurs earlier in the employee's tenure.

Another cost that leadership must factor in when calculating turnover cost, is productivity loss due to turnover, although difficult to quantify and measure (White, 1995; Tracey & Hinkin, 2008). According to Tracey and Hinkin (2008) productivity loss are opportunity costs, and accounts for 70% of the total cost of turnover within most organizations. Kacmar et al. (2006) noted that the food industry is greatly affected by productivity loss, especially when new hires are learning their roles. Opportunity costs are missed sales (Tracey & Hinkin), which could have generated revenue had there been a fully staffed department. New employees are prone to make mistakes during training which causes waste in the food industry

(Kacmar, et al., 2006). Seasoned employees and line managers invest time into training and developing newly hired employees, making it nearly impossible to generate sales or service customers. As noted by Kacmar et al., turnover negatively impacts business units and organizational success. When turnover increases in a department, the performance of the department and organization profitability decreases.

Turnover is a serious concern for organizations as it disrupts workflow and increases expenditures. White (1995) noted that it cost the fast food industry $500 to replace one crew member and $1500 to replace a manager. As illustrated by White, if a fast food company needs 300 crew members for operational purposes and experience 200% turnover, then the annual cost will be $30,000. 300 x 200% = 600 new hires. Therefore to maintain 300 employees at a loss of 200% turnover, the company must hire 600 crew members to operate at full staff and maintain efficiency.

Summary

There is no specific literature on recruiting and its influence on satisfaction as measured by morale; performance; and turnover. However, current research provides substantial information on how the variables can stimulate or decrease each other when growth opportunities are lacking. Research has revealed that employees' desire growth and the lack of it mitigated by other factors can decrease satisfaction, morale, stagnate performance, and stimulate turnover. As noted by Westover et al. (2010) absenteeism, performance, and turnover are correlated to job satisfaction. Through an effective selection process, leadership can offer growth opportunities to their workforce, specifically, high performing employees. Growth is achieved through promotions, challenging assignments, additional responsibilities, etc., and when these opportunities are offered to employees with growth needs satisfaction will increase.

When leadership affords employees opportunities to develop professionally, satisfaction ensues. Asvir et al. (2011) noted that an organization with a competitive edge has competent and satisfied workforce. A satisfied workforce is productive and strives to attain organizational goals. The workforce shares the organizations vision, is receptive to customer needs, productive and increases efficiency. Dissatisfaction is eminent when leadership fails to recognize what their workforce values, and does not provide developmental opportunities to them.

Dissatisfaction with the job or factors associated with the job decreases morale. A decrease in morale causes employees to develop a negative attitude towards the work environment. Consequently employees think of quitting and or turnovers occurs. Turnover is a never-ending problem that Human Resources effortlessly try to curtail. Westover et al. (2010) noted that turnover is very costly to businesses. To reduce turnover, leadership must develop programs and practices that foster retention. Schoenherr (2009) indicated that retaining high performers is cost effective, because it is expensive to replace high performing employees when they leave.

Leadership must acknowledge the values of their employees and make all possible efforts to meet those needs and consequently increase satisfaction. Leadership should give current employees opportunities to interview and receive promotions instead of recruiting new employees from outside the organization. As noted by White (1995) organizations with ineffective selection process experience high turnover. Such organizations seek to recruit externally without using the proper measures to screen the candidates. Giving internal employees opportunities to interview, and obtain promotions, increases employee commitment, and prevents selection blunders due to incomplete background checks. Internal employees will commit to leadership and organizational vision, when they recognize that they are valued and are rewarded for their hard work through promotions.

*A **little side note**: if you enjoy analyzing numerical data and reviewing research jargon – then you will enjoy Chapters 3 (deals with research methodology) and 4 (centers on data analysis). It is recommended that you review the themes (such as emotions, performance, willingness to go to work, etc.) that emerged from during data analysis and interpretation in Chapter 4. This can be found on pages 65 to 70. If you don't like to deal with percentages or ratios, then feel free and review the Summary of Research Findings (pages 72 – 77) then continue to Chapter 5 to learn about restructuring or revamping your current ineffective process.*

CHAPTER THREE
What Methodology is Applicable?

The purpose of the research was to perform a qualitative examination, and explore the shared experiences of internal candidates who have participated in the recruiting and selection process. The researcher's ontological assumption steered the decision to conduct a qualitative study with the intention of understanding the phenomenon. Realities of participants are subjective and multiple (Creswell, 2007), and are projections of participants imagination (Morgan & Smircich, 1980). Hence, though the experiences of participants were slightly dissimilar, the researcher identified the common shared experiences of participants.

Miles and Huberman (1984) noted that qualitative studies yield rich textural descriptions and explanations from participants. The relationship between internal recruiting, job satisfaction, morale, job performance, and employee turnover was examined to ascertain satisfaction or dissatisfaction with the recruiting process and its influence on the aforementioned variables. Additionally, the effects of the recruiting process on intent to leave were assessed. The research questions which were addressed in this qualitative study were:

1. Is there a significant difference in employee satisfaction after they experience the recruiting and selection process?
2. Is there a significant difference in employee morale (as measured by tardiness and absenteeism) after they experience the recruiting and selection process?
3. Is there a significant difference in employee performance after they experience the recruiting and selection process?
4. Has intent to leave or turnover increased after employees experience the recruiting and selection process?

Research Design

This phenomenological study attempted to describe the shared experiences of employees who had participated in the recruiting and selection process. According to Creswell (2009) phenomenological research identifies the real meaning of a phenomenon that has been experienced and described by participants. The objective was to understand the perceptions of employees when they: applied for positions; obtained interviews; obtained promotions; received follow up communications, or lack of it after each process. Van Manen (2006) indicated that phenomenological research focuses on describing meanings of the phenomenon.

According to Moustakas (1994), what participants experienced and how participants experienced the phenomenon should be described. Creswell (2007) noted that it is necessary to get a good understanding of the shared phenomenon in order to develop policies or practices. Human Resources will be provided with a keen insight on the shared experienced phenomenon and how it can be reduced so as to: increase satisfaction; performance; morale; and also curtail intent to leave and turnover. Creswell (2007) indicated that phenomenological research describes the common lived experiences of participants.

Although there are two types of phenomenological research: hermeneutical, and transcendental (Creswell, 2007), the current study utilized the transcendental approach. The researcher collected accurate and detailed information so as to richly describe the experiences of participants. Moustakas (1994) indicated that using the transcendental approach requires the researcher to bracket their experiences and remain objective. Thus, the researcher: disclosed her experiences with the recruiting and selection process; set it aside (Creswell, 2007), remained objective; collected and analyzed data without bias.

The researcher has worked in Talent Acquisition, Recruiting and Human Resources for approximately 20 years, and has recruited for various roles and functions within multiple and diverse organizations. The researcher prevented her own experiences from overshadowing her perspectives as it relates to the phenomenon, and the lived experiences of the participants. The researcher set aside her experiences in Human Resources when she asked participants about their own experiences to the phenomenon, and how their experiences influenced their satisfaction, morale, performance and intent to leave.

The researcher spent two weeks collecting data through in-depth phone interviews with open-ended questions. Creswell (2009) posits that the primary source of data gathering in a phenomenological research is through interviews; however, observations and reviewing of documents can also be utilized. After data was collected, it was analyzed with the assistance of qualitative software. Categories and subcategories were created as a result of coding, and patterns and themes of the shared experiences emerged.

Selection of Participants

Criterion sampling was used in the research to understand participants' experiences to the phenomenon. Creswell (2007) noted that criterion sampling is suitable in studies where selected participants meet some criterion or have experienced the phenomenon. Hence, participants were purposefully selected. The sample comprised of 20 employees who had been selected purposefully in a non-random method from the finance, accounting and other administrative departments. There were two distinct groups: group one comprised of 10 participants who had experienced the phenomenon only once; and group two comprised of 10 participants who had experienced the phenomenon more than once. Participants in both groups had applied for managerial and director positions. This sample consisted of employees who were not selected for promotions or transfers at one or more points in their career. Although some of these participants had since obtained some promotions since their initial dissatisfaction with the process, the interview questions required them to reflect on the time when they were not selected for a promotion. According to Labuschagne (2003) qualitative studies results in a wealth of data from a small a sample. As noted by Creswell, purposeful sampling allows the researcher to deliberately select specific people who can best provide the researcher with information about the central phenomenon. The study was conducted with employees within an organization who had gone through the recruiting process.

The researcher partnered with an administrative staff at the selected organization. The organization had various offices across the United States and employed professionals with college degrees. To ensure the privacy and protection of participants, the researcher: signed a confidentiality agreement form, stating that sensitive information will not be shared; and ensured that all emails containing employee information were protected. To ensure that participants met established criterion, the administrative staff member held a meeting with a large group. In the meeting, employees were informed of the purpose of the research and requirement for participation. The requirements were: a minimum of one year of employment for participation; and having had an experience with the recruiting and selection process to obtain promotional growth. According to Creswell (2007) criterion sampling is useful and strong in quality assurance.

Instrumentations

This phenomenological study utilized interviews as the only data collection method. Creswell (2009) posits that researchers build rapport with participants and explore issues, with the intention of gathering sufficient data that can be used to develop the patterns of the shared experiences. Participants were interviewed on the phone and asked to reflect on: what happened, how it happened, and how they felt when it happened. The researcher took detailed notes with a pen and paper. Phone interviews were audio recorded for later transcription. Creswell (2009) indicated that interviews are effective when the researcher is unable to observe participants directly as events occur. The goal of the research was to understand the common shared experience of employees who had experienced the recruiting and selection process within the organization. Due to the fact that the experiences occurred in the past, the researcher was unable to observe any occurrences. Thus the in-depth interviews with open-ended questions allowed participants to unveil and recall historical information.

The interviews included sensory questions that triggered memories which revealed how participants felt about the experience; and how that experience consequently decreased or increased satisfaction, performance, morale and turnover. Some of the sensory questions pertained to how participants "felt" when they: applied for available positions; obtained interviews or the lack of interviews; obtained promotions or the lack of promotions; and follow up communications after each process. According to Harris and Guillemin (2012) asking participants questions that encompasses the senses allows participants to recall strong memories or feelings. Such questions aid participants to reflect on: what happened; how it happened; and how participants felt when it happened.

Recalling strong memories provides additional insight as to how the experienced phenomenon resulted in attitudinal and behavioral changes. All participants' privacy was respected, such that if they choose not to answer questions that will invoke unpleasant memories, the researcher skipped those questions. Participants were giving information that highlighted and explained the purpose and benefits of the study, including any related risks with the aim of giving participants the right to withdraw from the research without reprisals or penalties.

After interviews were conducted with participants, the researcher analyzed gathered data. Labuschagne (2003) noted that qualitative analysis comprises of organizing non-numerical data into patterns and themes. Miles and Huberman (1984) noted that coding is data reduction whereby the researcher simplifies and transforms data in field notes. Creswell (2009) posits that the researcher first review the raw data that has been collected from participants. Direct quotations obtained from participants through in-depth interviews were analyzed and categorized into major themes. According to Labuschagne (2003) direct quotations from participants describe their experiences, feelings, opinions, and allow others to understand their world. After data was categorized into major themes, a textural description (Creswell, 2007) was written to describe how participants experienced the central phenomenon.

Methodological Assumptions or Limitations

This phenomenological study utilized interviews as the only means of data collection. It was assumed that participants who were uncomfortable with sensory questions chose not to answer some questions (Harris & Guillemin, 2012). Some of the limitations of the study included: inability to review attendance records, exit interviews and performance appraisals;

inability to generalize the findings to a larger population or different industries; reluctance of employees to respond to questions pertaining to intent to leave; and inconsistency of interviewee responses.

Due to proprietary reasons attendance records and exit interviews could not be reviewed. The researcher was unable to review attendance records to measure: tardiness and absenteeism, before and after an experience with the recruiting and selection process. This limitation prevented the researcher from accurately measuring the attendance of participants before and after an experience to the phenomena. By not reviewing exit interviews, the researcher could not determine if voluntary turnovers were the result of dissatisfaction to the phenomena. As a result of not reviewing past performance measurements the researcher could not ascertain whether participants were high or low performers prior to an experience with the phenomenon. By knowing the performance ranking of participants a comparative analysis could have revealed a difference in performance prior to and after the phenomenon. The difference if any, could have helped explained whether dissatisfaction with the phenomenon affected performance or not.

Although generalizability was a limitation, the researcher undertook several procedures to bolster validity and reliability. According to Creswell (2009) reliability can boost qualitative research during the coding process. To ensure consistency in the definition of codes, data was compared with codes developed by the researcher and cross-checked with codes developed by other researchers. In addition, collected data was cross checked with information from literature reviews to ensure consistency.

Qualitative validity was achieved through reflexivity. Reflexivity increased the validity of the study, because the researcher examined any personal biases, values, and experiences as an employee and a recruiter. As noted by Hsiung (2008) reflexivity is a process whereby the researcher does self-examination to ascertain why they are conducting the specific research, and what they desire to attain. The researcher has been in Talent Acquisition and Human Resources for approximately 20 years, and has recruited for various roles and functions within multiple organizations. The researcher ensured that data analysis and interpretation of data was not affected by pre-existing biases. The researcher prevented her own experiences from overshadowing her perspectives as it relates to the phenomenon, and the lived experiences of the participants. The researcher set aside her experiences in her field and asked participants about their own experiences to the phenomenon, and how their experiences influenced their satisfaction, morale, performance and intent to leave. As noted by Watts (2007), it is imperative that the researcher specifies their intentions for conducting the study.

Procedures

The researcher submitted a letter to the leadership within the organization requesting permission to conduct a study with their employees. The letter stipulated reasons for the study, and the organizational benefits that can be obtained from the study. An IRB application was completed and sent to the Argosy University's Internal Review board to approve before studies could be initiated. The application highlighted: purpose of the study; methodology; informed consent; treatment of participants; maintenance of interview notes; potential benefits of the study, etc. Once the board evaluated and approved the project, the researcher commenced with the study.

Data Collection

Single interviews were conducted with each participant on the phone. Participants were asked six open-ended questions about their experience to the phenomenon. (Creswell, 2009) recommended that researchers ask four to five open ended questions. Four questions centered around what was experienced and how they were influenced by it (Creswell, 2007), and the other two questions incorporated the senses to enrich the lived experiences. According to Harris and Guillemin (2012) applying sensory awareness in interview questions allows the participant to unlock memories and provide information on their feelings and beliefs as it pertains to their experience. The following questions were asked:

1. Discuss your satisfaction after you went through the recruiting and selection process for a promotional opportunity.
2. Discuss how you felt after you went through the recruiting and selection process.

3. How did the experience affect your desire to go to work every day of the week?
4. Discuss how your production and efficiency was affected after you experienced the recruiting and selection process.
5. Discuss how you felt about your employment after you went through the recruiting and selection process.
6. Describe your desire to stay within the organization after you experienced the recruiting and selection process.

Direct quotations from the interviews were recorded by taking handwritten notes in a notebook, and by audiotaping, to ensure that responses are recorded accurately. According to Labuschagne (2003) direct quotations are raw data that divulges participant's experiences, feelings, and thoughts about the phenomenon. Transcribing direct quotes allowed the researcher to establish patterns and themes during data analysis. Creswell (2009) advised that researchers utilize an interview protocol for qualitative interviews which should include: an ice breaker; probing questions; and a thank you statement after the interview.

Data Processing and Analysis

Data analysis allowed the researcher to look beyond the raw data, and analyze the data to gain understanding and meaning. According to Labuschagne (2003) conducting an in-depth qualitative analysis provides richness, understanding and meaning to participants experiences. During the analysis process the researcher organized, categorized, and coded data gathered from the interviews. Creswell (2009) noted that in data analysis the researcher analyzes raw data that has been collected from participants. Creswell indicated that the process of data collection and data analysis in a qualitative study should be simultaneous.

Creswell (2007) posits that the researcher should perform constant comparative method of analysis, where the researcher begins analysis when data is been collected. Through analysis of data obtained from the in-depth interviews, an understanding and meaning emerges Labuschagne (2003). This helps the researcher to compare data to emerging categories. The researcher also compared data from audio recordings and hand written notes before analysis begun to ensure consistency. Data obtained from participants were organized and entered into a computer software program for coding.

According to Creswell (2009) coding allows the researcher to categorize all gathered data. As noted by Miles and Huberman (1968) coding reduces raw data or direct quotes from interviews into simple themes or patterns. Labuschagne (2003) indicated that through content analysis, collected data are organized into themes. The researcher selected an open coding or major categories, and then focused on an identified core phenomenon in axial coding (Creswell, 2007). Afterwards, various sub categories was identified and interconnected or interrelated to form the selective coding (Creswell, 2007). Finally, the interconnections of selected codes formed various themes or a story about the commonalities of lived experiences. The researcher then wrote a descriptive report on the shard lived experiences of participants.

The researcher investigated various Computer Assisted Data Analysis Software (CADAS): MAXQDA; Atlas.ti; HyperRESEARCH; and NVIVO 8. All the identified software programs were PC based programs, that imports transcribed data for coding, however they differed in cost and ease of use. MAXQDA had great functionalities and capabilities. It appeared to be easy to use after a brief tutorial, and it was also cost effective. Atlas.ti. was efficient and provided programs for analysis; however, it was slightly expensive. HyperRESEARCH allowed the researcher to select from a code book, nonetheless after a brief tutorial; the researcher concluded that HyperRESEARCH was not user friendly. NVIVO 8 was user friendly, provided great tutorial, and was cost effective. The researcher decided to use MAXQDA because it was free for the first 30 days. MAXQDA was effective and efficient in assisting the researcher to perform analysis in order to derive the rich themes and patterns that emerged from gathered data.

CHAPTER FOUR

What were the Results of the Study?

This qualitative study was conducted to ascertain a clear understanding of the perceptions of employees when they: apply for positions; obtain interviews; obtain promotions; receive follow-up communications, or lack of it after each process. Twenty professionals from the finance, accounting and other administrative departments within a single organization were phone interviewed, and asked six open-ended questions. The questions focused on how the recruiting and selection process influenced their satisfaction, morale, performance, and intent to leave or stay within the organization.

Were the Goals Achieved?

The goals and objectives was to gain a better understanding of the shared experiences of internal candidates who had participated in the recruiting and selection process. The study examined employee satisfaction, and or dissatisfaction with the recruiting and selection process. In addition, the study examined how an experience with the phenomenon influenced: attitude towards their job; attitude towards their work environment; performance; and decisions to leave the organization. The study provides information to leaders about mitigating factors that affects employee satisfaction and increases intent to leave and consequently turnover.

This chapter provides detailed information on the process of data collection and analysis on "what" and "how" the phenomenon was experienced. The formation of categories and subcategories was incorporated to provide a clear description of how interrelated themes emerged as a result of coding. Themes from participants' subjective statements and its meanings concerning the issue were highlighted to demonstrate the commonality of the experienced phenomenon.

Were the Research Questions Answered?

The significant meanings of statements that form themes were intended to answer the research questions. The interview questions *(found under Data Collection in Chapter 3)* were created to answer the research questions. The results are explained in this chapter *(under: Discussion of Interview Questions).*

Did Collected Data Measure the Variables?

To gain access to the rich data that was collected for the study, the researcher sent a written permission letter to the Vice President of the selected organization. The letter explained the research purpose, the process of data collection, and the potential benefits to the organization. The letter also indicated that data from the research will be treated confidentially and handled securely, where results will be reported as an aggregate summary only. After permission was granted, a pre-identified administrator coordinated between the researcher and potential participants.

The pre-identified administrator held a meeting with approximately 60 employees to inform them of the study. The researcher then sent a signed informed consent form via email to the administrator who distributed it to the finance, accounting and other departments within the administrative group, where the sample was obtained. Employees who wanted to participate in the study signed the informed consent form and forwarded it to the researcher via email, then followed up with a phone call to schedule a phone interview. Out of the 60 employees informed of the study, 20 responded to the researcher.

During the phone interview process, the researcher assured each participant of confidentiality and anonymity. Prior to asking the interview questions, participants were asked to state their: name; current job title; the number of times they have applied for positions; the specific positions applied for; and the number of years with the company. Participants were asked six open-ended questions which emphasized their satisfaction with the recruiting and selection process; and how it influenced their morale, performance and desire to stay within the organization. Participants were asked to reflect on: what happened, how it happened, and how they felt when it happened.

Demographic Information

Data was collected from March 8 through March 22, 2013. Data was obtained from 20 professionals through phone interviews. 13 participants were men and 7 were women. All participants were over 18 years of age, and knowledge of specific ages was not necessary for this study. The organization is an equal employment employer and attracts professionals of all ages. The educational background of participants ranged from a Bachelor Degree to a Doctoral Degree. 9 participants were in clerical, non-managerial positions, 9 were in line management positions, and 2 were directors. Participants had been with the organization from a minimum of 1.5 years to a maximum of 7 years. To be precise, 30% of the participants had been there up to a maximum of 3 years; 25% had been there for 3.5 years and 45% had been there from 4 to 7 years.

Data Analysis

The data analysis phase was aided by the use of a qualitative software program called MAXQDA 11. Responses from each participant that was collected during the interview phase was scanned and saved on Adobe pdf. After which the pdf files were exported into MAXQDA 11 for analysis. After data was converted into MAXQDA 11, each participant's information was saved under their name. The researcher then initiated the process of creating codes based on interview questions and responses. As similar codes were created based on participant responses, categories and subcategories were created by the researcher. After coding, the researcher identified common themes from participant's responses based on the frequency of codes. Codes and variables created from the raw data, and obtained from demographics were exported into both HTML and Excel for graphic display. The graphic display and charts were necessary to boost the researcher's description of the experienced phenomenon. The following are major themes that emerged from each interview question.

Interview Question 1: Discuss your satisfaction after you went through the recruiting and selection process for a promotional opportunity?

Q1 Theme 1 – Satisfied with the entire process

Q1 Theme 2 – The entire process needs improvement

Q1 Theme 3 – Frustrated with the entire process

Q1 Theme 4 – Not satisfied with the entire process

Q1 Theme 5 – Feedback received from leadership lacked details

Q1 Theme 6 – There was a lack of feedback from leadership

Q1 Theme 7 – Feedback from leadership was negative

Figure 3 is a graphic representation of the common themes that emerged from question 1.

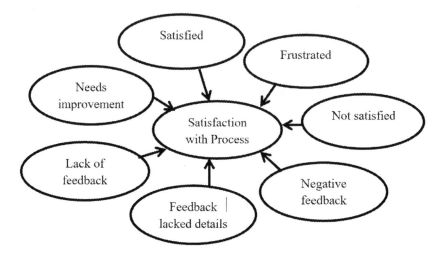

Figure 3. **Satisfaction with Recruiting and Selection Process**

Interview Question 2: Discuss how you felt after you went through the recruiting and selection process?

Q2 Theme 1 – Felt good after going through the process

Q2 Theme 2 – Felt miserable after going through the process

Q2 Theme 3 – Felt sad after going through the process

Q2 Theme 4 – Felt disillusioned after going through the process

Q2 Theme 5 – Was upset after going through the process

Q2 Theme 6 – Was hopeful after going through the process

Figure 4 is a graphic representation of the common themes that emerged from question 2.

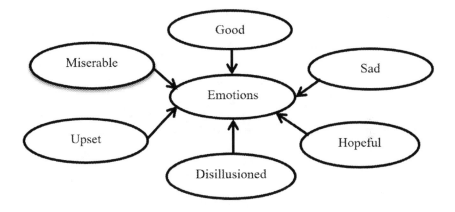

Figure 4. **Emotions after Experience with Recruiting and Selection Process**

Interview Question 3: How did the experience affect your desire to go to work every day of the week?

Q3 Theme 1 – Was motivated to go back to work

Q3 Theme 2 – Was unmotivated to go back to work

Q3 Theme 3 - Was unaffected by the process and leaderships' decision

Q3 Theme 4 – Found it difficult to go to work afterwards

Figure 5 is a graphic representation of the common themes that emerged from question 3.

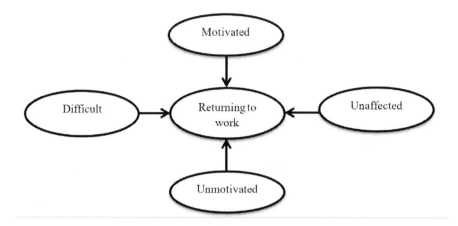

Figure 5. **Returning to Work after Experience with Recruiting and Selection Process**

Interview Question 4: Discuss how your production and efficiency was affected after you experienced the recruiting and selection process?

Q4 Theme 1 – Overall performance stayed the same

Q4 Theme 2 – There was a lack of fervor to perform

Q4 Theme 3 – Overall performance increased

Q4 Theme 4 – Overall performance was minimally affected

Q4 Theme 5 – There was a decrease in the quality of servicing clients / customers

Q4 Theme 6 – Overall performance plummeted

Figure 6 is a graphic representation of the common themes that emerged from question 4.

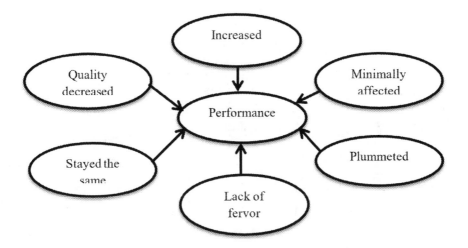

Figure 6. **Performance after Experience with Recruiting and Selection Process**

Interview Question 5: Discuss how you felt about your employment after you went through the recruiting and selection process

Q5 Theme 1 - Feels that there are opportunities within organization

Q5 Theme 2 – Feels loyalty towards organization

Q5 Theme 3 – Feels good about current employment /employer

Q5 Theme 4 – Has intentions of leaving organization

Figure 7 is a graphic representation of the common themes that emerged from question 3.

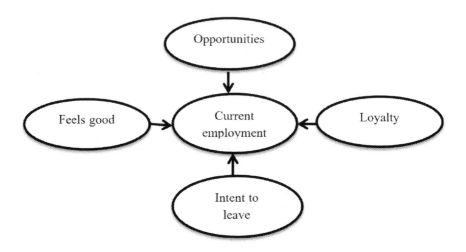

Figure 7. **Feelings about Employment after Experience with Process**

Interview Question 6: Describe your desire to stay within the organization after you experienced the recruiting and selection process.

Q6 Theme 1 - Wants to stay

Q6 Theme 2 – Wants to leave

Figure 8 is a graphic representation of the common themes that emerged from question 3.

Figure 8. **Intent to leave after Experience with Recruiting and Selection Process**

Discussion of Interview Questions

The interview questions posed to participants yielded similar responses which were reflected in the major themes. Although there were commonalities in the experienced phenomenon, there were some underlining factors that were unique. Question 1 focused on satisfaction with the recruiting and selection process. This question aroused experiences from participants from as early as their first experience with the process. Most participants had been employed with the organization and had previously obtained promotions, but their recent experience had been negative. Nevertheless, the recent experience did not thwart their previous experience, thus yielding a positive experience. Others had applied for more than seven positions and had not obtained promotion, nor were they giving substantial reason for a decline, thus yielding a negative experience.

Out of the 20 participants 35% were either: satisfied or happy. 3%r felt that the recruiting and selection process was good. 17% of the participants wanted the process to be improved for the enhancement of skills, and to improve feedback. 45% of the participants were dissatisfied with the process. These participants were either: disappointed; disturbed; or frustrated because they were not giving the opportunity to go through the entire recruiting and selection process. These participants did not receive feedback after they submitted applications, or they participated in the first round of interviews; however, they were not selected to participate in the second round of interviews.

Communication was a major theme that resonated with almost all participants regardless of their satisfaction or dissatisfaction with the recruiting and selection process. 90% of participants indicated that the communication from leadership during the process: lacked detail; was absent; inadequate; was negative; was dishonest; or was delayed. 10% of participants felt that communication with leadership was either good or fair. The feedback process seemed to have increased participants dissatisfaction, frustration and disappointment with the process. The feedback process was not detailed, constructive, and immediate.

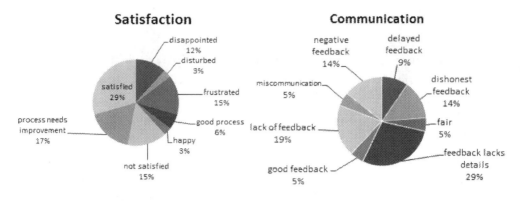

Satisfaction

Communication

Figure 9. **Analysis of Themes that Emerged from Question 1**

Although a large percentage of participants were satisfied with the process, the responses were very different for question 2. Interview question 2 focused on participants' emotions after they experienced the recruiting and selection process. This question elicited feelings from instances when participants did not: progress through the process; receive follow through from decision makers; or receive adequate feedback. 63% of participants were: discouraged, disillusioned, miserable, sad, upset, or angry about the experience. 5% of participants were surprised about the process and did not know how to feel about it. Conversely 32% of participants were either happy, felt good about the process, or were hopeful of getting a promotion in the future.

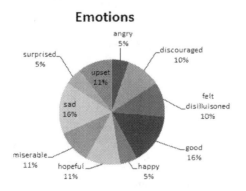

Emotions

Figure 10. **Analysis of Themes that Emerged from Question 2**

The emotions experienced after the recruiting and selection appeared to be a determinant in participant's desire to go to work every day of the week.

Four major themes emerged from question 3, which illustrated a pattern from previously asked questions on satisfaction and emotions. 12% of participants found it difficult to go to work, and 19% were unmotivated to go to work the first week after experiencing the process. These participants felt that leadership had: been unfair with their decisions; had not provided information on what participants can do to improve the skills; or that leadership had been disloyal. After hours and days of ill emotions these participants returned to work, because it was their source of income.

Another theme that emerged was the motivation to go back to work. 44% of the participants were motivated to go, not because they were all satisfied with the process. Rather, some of these participants had been declined second round interviews and or promotions, yet they wanted to prove management wrong. Ironically, they felt empowered by leaderships' decision although the decision did not yield a promotion. Hence, these participants went back to work with a great attitude, to work harder. 25% of the participants were unaffected with the process, regardless of their satisfaction level. As a result, these participants went back to work and continued to operate in their usual manner.

Returning to Work

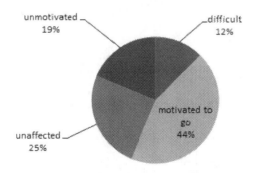

Figure 11. **Analysis of Themes that Emerged from Question 3**

Returning to work after experiencing the phenomenon did not necessarily mean that participants were satisfied enough to perform, on the contrary. Themes that emerged from question 4 demonstrate that participants were at work; however performance was not up to par. The question asked participants to discuss how their production and efficiency was affected after they experienced the recruiting and selection process. 41% of participants indicated that their performance stayed the same. Therefore, although they went to work after dissatisfaction with the phenomenon, these participants did not change their production output and quality of service. 27% of participants lacked fervor to work. These participants did not work as hard to problem solve, and it took more effort to perform their daily tasks. 9% of the participants experienced a decrease in quality. These participants were not quick to return calls to clients or follow through with clients as expected.

The performance of 5% of the participants plummeted, such that both quality and quantity of work was problematic. 9% of participants' performances were minimally affected whereby their quality and quantity of output did not decline significantly. Of all the respondents, only 9% increased their performance. This occurred for two reasons: they were motivated to work on specific things that were mentioned in the feedback that they received; or because declined participants wanted to work hard to show leadership that they had made a wrong decision for not promoting them.

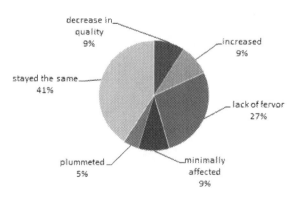

Performance

Figure 12. **Analysis of Themes that Emerged from Question 4**

Increasing performance was important to participants who wanted to continue their employment with the organization. Remarkable most participants who did not increase their performance also wanted to continue their employment with the organization. Themes that developed in questions 5 revealed that most participants were content with their employer and employment. Question 5 focused on how participants felt about their employment after they went through the recruiting and selection process. 37% of respondents indicated that they felt there were opportunities with their current employer. 26% revealed that they had loyalty to their employer even though they believed that leadership did not have loyalty towards them. 21% of the participants felt good about their employment. 11% indicated that they had intentions of leaving. Some of the participants who felt good and believed that they had opportunities with their employer, alluded to feeling valued, and having equity with the organization. Conversely, all the respondents who had intentions of leaving, and some of those who had loyalty to the organization also referred to feeling unappreciated and being devalued. Participants' view of their current employment also yielded information on their feelings towards their employer.

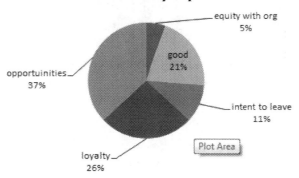

Figure 13. **Analysis of Themes that Emerged from Question 5**

Feeling undervalued and unappreciated caused many respondents to think of quitting and seek after other employments, as a result of not getting a promotion. Question 6 required participants to discuss their desire to stay within the organization after they experienced the recruiting and selection process. Two major themes were unearthed from this question. 40% of the respondents wanted to leave and 60% wanted to stay. Participants who wanted to leave had: applied for opportunities with other competitors; or had not applied for opportunities but were ready to leave if the competitor called.

Intent

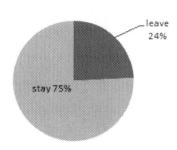

Figure 14. **Analysis of Themes that Emerged from Question 6**

The participants who wanted to stay did so for varying reasons. Some of these participants calculated the risk of leaving versus staying. Some were concerned about the market and its stability, thus they preferred to stay with their current employer and in their current situation. Others wanted to stay with their employer because they were the main source of income provider for their family, and did not want to start a new employment where their income might be reduced. There were still others who wanted to stay because they had made friends within the organization and the social network was very important to them. Some participants liked the proximity of their work to their house. And there were participants who wanted to stay because they were satisfied with their employer, were content with their employer, or were hopeful of a good career with their employer.

Validity and Reliability

To ensure that this phenomenological study was valid, the researcher guarded against bias, and checked for accuracy throughout the phases of data collection, analysis and interpretation. The use of peer examination (Creswell, 2009) to review the entire process was adhered to. To bolster reliability, codes were systematically compared to data to establish consistency. According to Creswell (2007), qualitative researchers should collect valid and credible information. The researcher ensured that the raw data obtained was not made up, but rather credible by using an audio phone recorder. According to Maxwell (1992) this process is termed descriptive validity. Every response from each participant was captured accurately with the use of an audio device to ward against erroneous transcribing.

Participants' perception towards the experienced phenomenon and the words they used was not diluted by the researcher. Maxwell (1992) noted that for a study to be valid there has to be interpretive validity, whereby the researcher captures participants' perception and "communicative meaning" (p288). In this study, interpretive validity was achieved when participants were asked a series of questions about their feelings towards the experienced phenomenon and how it influenced them. Responses from participants were reiterated to ensure that the researcher captured participants intended meanings for each question.

Reflexivity is important in a qualitative study, as it helps increase the validity of the study. Creswell (2007) postulated that researchers remain reflexive throughout the study, and Hsiung (2008) advised that the researcher perform self-examination to ascertain reasons for conducting the specific research, and desired results. Reflexivity was achieved because the researcher was aware of her own biases and bracketed her experiences to remain objective. With respect to the effects of internal recruiting on satisfaction, morale, performance and turnover, the researcher believed that satisfaction will decrease. After 14 years in the recruiting and Human Resources profession, the researcher believed the following: satisfaction, morale and performance will be low; and turnover will be high. By setting aside this belief, the researcher approached data collection, analysis, and interpretation objectively without bias.

Summary of Research Findings

Research questions were posed in this study to understand the common shared and lived experiences of employees who had participated in the recruiting process to obtain a promotion. Responses to the research questions were necessary to provide leadership with information that can aid them in: revamping the current recruiting and selection process to increase satisfaction, morale, performance and decrease turnover.

During the selection process, two groups were identified. Group one comprised of 10 participants who had gone through the recruiting and selection process only one time, because they had applied for one position prior to this research. Group two comprised of 10 participants who had had applied for multiple positions since they started their employment. Group two had either been interviewed for all positions applied for, or for some of them. In either respect, participants in group two had been rejected multiple times before obtaining a promotion, if any. Participants from both groups had applied for director, managerial and non-managerial positions. The director positions managed line supervisors and the entire department. The managerial positions supervised the clerical staff, and the non-managerial positions were individual contributors. To be specific, 20% of participants applied for non-managerial positions, 95% applied for managerial positions and 20% applied for director positions.

Results from the six interview questions revealed that most participants in group one were more satisfied with the recruiting and selection process than those in group two. Some of these employees had been with their employer for two years or less and were in clerical positions. They thought that the process was good and were receptive to the feedback received. Most of these participants had applied for managerial positions, and others had applied for clerical positions but with more responsibilities and challenging assignments. These participants believed the reason for not obtaining a promotion stemmed from the fact that they lacked the skills needed to supervise or coach a team. As a result, morale for participants who were satisfied in group one was not as affected. Instead they were motivated to go back to work. These participants were eager to develop the skills needed to acquire future promotions. They were optimistic and hopeful of growth advancement within the organization. These were participants who had no intentions of leaving the organization.

Conversely, a few of the participants in group one were not as satisfied with the outcome of interviews. They believed that they had some skills that could add value to the department, and were not receptive to feedback from leadership. These participants asserted to the vague feedback received, which did not identify specific areas in their skills that needed to be developed. They expected leadership and decision makers in the recruiting process to offer some form of training and development but that was not forthcoming. Satisfaction with these participants was low; they were upset, and found it difficult to return to work. When they went to work they kept their performance at the same level and saw no reason to increase production. Despite the fact that they performance stayed the same they wanted to remain with the employer, and seek after future opportunities.

Results for participants in group two showed that most of the participants were dissatisfied with the recruiting and selection process. Participants in this group had been with the organization for more than 3 years and had applied to numerous positions without much progress. Some were in clerical positions, and a few were in managerial positions. These participants applied for mostly managerial and director positions. Participants were frustrated and disappointed with the process. Some of these employees performed their manager's daily task when the mangers were out sick or on vacation. These participants asserted that leadership prompted them to apply for managerial or director positions, yet they did not receive the promotions. Some assumed that they were allowed to participate in the first round of interviews for the purpose of formality, instead of an opportunity to discuss their knowledge, skills and abilities. They believed that the feedback received for being rejected was either negative or dishonest. Employees in this group felt disillusioned, discouraged and upset, because they were encouraged to apply for upper level positions that did not materialize into promotions. Some did not trust leadership, because they believed that leadership had their own network of employees that they promoted to senior level positions. They felt devalued and unappreciated. Some were unmotivated, to go to work, decreased, performance and had intentions to quit. Others were motivated to go to work, kept performance at an average level, and had intentions of staying in the organization because they needed the job and income.

Research Question 1 addressed the difference in employee satisfaction after they experienced the recruiting and selection process. Through the use of open-ended interview questions, the researcher was able to obtain rich and detailed information on participants' satisfaction and mitigating factors. Satisfaction level decreased as some employees kept going through the process over a period of months and years without obtaining a promotion. Factors that decreased satisfaction were attributed to the communication process, where feedback was inadequate or was not helpful to the employee.

Research Question 2 focused on employee morale (as measured by tardiness and absenteeism) after they experienced the recruiting and selection process. Responses obtained from the interviews provided information on morale since attendance records could not be reviewed. After experiencing the phenomenon, participants who were dissatisfied with the process were initially distraught, discouraged, and or miserable. As a result, their initial response was to stay home for a couple of days and not show up to work. Some of these participants choose to be late for work and others missed work for a day or two. Yet there were others who after the initial thought of staying home, decided against it and motivated themselves to return to work with a pleasant attitude. Some of the participants who were satisfied increased their morale with respect to tardiness or absenteeism. Satisfaction did prompt them to go to work early; and they maintained a happy attitude regardless of a promotion or lack of it.

Research Question 3 centered on measuring a marked difference in employee performance after they experienced the recruiting and selection process. Detailed information provided by participants revealed that dissatisfaction did influence performance, however it was not significant. Some employees who were dissatisfied with the process and, or did not obtain a promotion found it difficult to perform up to par. They either required more energy and motivation to perform, or they made mistakes and were not as efficient. Performance of some satisfied employees did not improve, but rather stayed the same, as these employees believed that their current production was satisfactory.

Research Question 4 focused on intent to leave and turnover after employees experienced the recruiting and selection process. Turnover could not be measured as the researcher was not permitted to review any documents of terminated employees. Information provided by respondents exposed the intentions of participants. Dissatisfaction with the process influenced the decisions of many participants who wanted to leave. Although the intention of leaving was entertained by most dissatisfied participants, few of them acted upon it by searching for new employments.

CHAPTER FIVE

What Have We Learnt?

Discussion

The recruiting process allows employees to attain growth, work on challenging assignments, ascertain their security within the firm, increase income, etc. For these reasons amongst others, employees choose to apply for positions that will yield the desired growth. Participants in the study were internal applicants and internal candidates who had expressed their interest in internally posted positions by: applying for a position(s) with completed applications, meeting the minimum qualification, and or proceeded through the interviewing process. The study analyzed employee satisfaction with the recruiting and selection process, and how it motivated or demotivated them to increase or decrease: morale; performance; and turnover.

The results of this study are intended to help organizational leaders acknowledge: that their current recruiting and selection process is not entirely satisfactory. Thus, the current process has the potential of increasing dissatisfaction. And with an increase in dissatisfaction, the impending decrease in morale and performance, and an increase in the intent to quit will persist. The study can help leadership to recognize that dissatisfaction exists, and provide an avenue to remedy the challenges of employee dissatisfaction.

The themes that were used to answer the research questions are to prove useful to leadership, should they recognize and acknowledge that dissatisfaction towards the recruiting and selection process exists. If Human Resources, Recruiting and other leaders accept that dissatisfaction due to the recruiting and selection process exists, they can strategically revamp the process and successfully: improve communication; provide every internal applicant and internal candidate an equal chance in the process to obtain growth opportunities; provide training to close gap in skills; and increase the commitment of employees to the organization. Human Resources can implement practices that are adhered to, and ensure an effective recruiting and selection process.

The study sought to answer four research questions which were valuable in assisting the researcher to understand the commonalities in experiences to the phenomena. Specific areas had to be investigated through the interview questions before the research questions could be answered. The research questions were:

Rq1 = Is there a significant difference in employee satisfaction after they experience the recruiting and selection process?

Rq2 =Is there a significant difference in employee morale (as measured by tardiness and absenteeism) after they experience the recruiting and selection process?

Rq3 = Is there a significant difference in employee performance after they experience the recruiting and selection process?

Rq4= Has intent to leave or turnover increased after employees experience the recruiting and selection process?

To answer the research questions, ample literature was reviewed. A phenomenological approach that utilized six open-ended questions was used to gain an insight of the lived and shared experiences of participants. Twenty employees were sampled and their responses were recorded, coded, and analyzed to capture the themes which formed a rich description of the commonalities in the experiences of the participants.

Common themes that emerged as a result of the open-ended interview questions formed the foundation in answering the research questions. The common themes developed from interview question one helped to answer research question one. The themes revealed that employee satisfaction decreased after experience with the phenomena, regardless of whether they had been rejected once or multiple times. Nevertheless, dissatisfaction was prevalent with employees who had gone through the process multiple times without success. Breakdowns in communication or lack of it appeared to increase dissatisfaction. The link between satisfaction with the process, and feedback about candidacy was crucial in shaping the feelings of employees towards their jobs. Participants expected and needed feedback on their candidacy as they wanted promotions and growth opportunities. The inefficiency of the process also aroused dissatisfaction, since employees were at a standstill in their endeavors to obtain growth. Literature on satisfaction supports these results as the lack of challenging assignments and growth opportunities negatively impacts satisfaction (Mahmood et al., 2011; Shaikh et al., 2012).

Common themes from interview question two and three assisted the researcher in answering research question two. From these themes, it was learnt that morale decreased for some participants and increased for others. Where there was a decrease, tardiness and absenteeism increased, though not for a lengthy period. These findings supports literature which asserts that: the relationship between morale and satisfaction is weak (George & Jones (2008), and that the relationship is strong (Tuzun, 2007; Cho & Perry, 2011; Kazi & Zadeh, 2011). Documents of attendance records could not be reviewed, however; participants asserted to being tardy, and or missing work for a couple of days.

Common themes from interview question four formed the premise for research question three where performance was moderately affected after experiencing the phenomena. Even though dissatisfaction was significantly high, performance did not decrease as expected. Instead, most participants' performance stayed the same or decreased but not drastically. Results revealed that the performance of: 41% stayed the same; 27% lacked fervor; 9% had a decrease in quality; 5% plummeted; 9% were minimally; and 9% increased. This supports research that affirms that the relationship between satisfaction and performance is moderate (Westover et al., 2010), and weak (Aydogdu & Asikgil, 2011). Participants who were satisfied barely increased their performance.

Literature stressing a strong correlation between satisfaction and turnover (Kazi & Zadeh, 2011) was not supported by the study, because turnover could not be measured. However interview questions five and six formed the foundation of simple themes that emerged to answer research question four. The themes pertained to participants desire to stay or quit despite their dissatisfaction. Some participants had loyalty towards their employer, others felt that there were potential opportunities within the organization, yet others felt it was better to leave the organization. Results revealed that: 75% of participants wanted to stay and 25% wanted to quit. This showed that regardless of the dissatisfaction, majority of participants wanted to stay within the organization.

The decision to stay was influenced by mitigating factors other than dissatisfaction. Findings support Mobley's (1977) assertion that the relationship between satisfaction and intent to leave is not a direct relationship. Mobley noted that when employees experience job dissatisfaction they follow a process whereby they: think of quitting; search and evaluate alternatives; compare alternatives to current situation; and make a decision. Participants were dissatisfied with the process; however, there were factors far more important that influenced their decision to stay instead of quit. The need for continuous income, current job security, equity within the organization, proximity to the job site etc., overshadowed dissatisfaction with the process. Risks were associated with intent to leave (Allen et al., 2007) and that made it unfavorable for employees to leave.

Conclusion

The purpose of the study was to ascertain an understanding of the significance of the recruiting and selection process to internal candidates. Meaning, how the process is able to influence the satisfaction level of employees and consequently affect their: attitudes towards their work; performance; and their decision to stay within the organization or leave. Understanding the relationship between the variables is vital in assisting leadership to revamp the current process. This study provided a unique contribution to the research on the relationship between satisfaction, morale, performance and turnover. The unique aspects are specific information attained from understanding the direct influence of the recruiting and selection process on satisfaction and morale, and the indirect influence on performance and turnover.

The recruiting and selection process is supposed to motivate employees to apply for job openings. The process should encourage applicants for growth attainments rather discourage them. Should employees lack the knowledge skills and abilities to obtain a promotion, it becomes leaderships' responsibility to invest in employees through training. This entire process encourages communication and improves satisfaction, and subsequently increases the value of the employee to the organization. Specific information that can improve the recruiting and selection process was attained from the qualitative interviews and also supported by current literature.

In chapter 2, literature was reviewed on the influence of satisfaction on promotion, morale, performance and intent to quit and turnover. By focusing on the afore mentioned variables and its correlation to the recruiting and selection process, current literature provided great insight on what leadership can do to increase satisfaction. Preenen et al. (2011) postulated that when employees work on challenging assignments, they increase their satisfaction. Challenging assignments can be obtained when employees are promoted. By applying for available opportunities, employees can go through the interviewing process and obtain promotions that will allow them to work on challenging assignments.

A decrease in satisfaction occurs when employees feel undervalued (Shaikh et al., 2012), and lack growth opportunities (Kazi & Zadeh, 2011). In the current research study, the inability to obtain growth and develop new skills infuriated employees after they participated in the recruiting and selection process. Several participants alluded to applying for multiple positions where they only received one interview and nothing happened afterwards. They were left to assume that they will be considered for positions that never materialized.

An effective process should provide all avenues including, thorough communication, and the availability of training and development programs (Preenen et al, 2011) necessary for growth attainment. Human Resources should revamp the recruiting and selection process, and ensure that internal applicants and internal candidates receive quick and honest feedback throughout the recruiting phase. Quarterly Performance Appraisals should be conducted with employees and established goals. In addition, leadership should develop training programs that enhances the knowledge and skills of employees who have been passed over for promotions. These training programs should be tied to established goals from the Quarterly Performance Appraisals, so that goals can be measured to ensure that employees are on target.

Morale was an important focus in the research since it is the attitude that employees have towards their work environment. It is vital for leadership to know about an employee's attitude towards their work, their team members, and leadership. Morale can determine: whether employees will choose to go to work or not; and if they go to work, how they will interact with team members to problem solve. Thus, an employee's satisfaction in relation to their morale is important for productivity and retention. Literature asserted that: satisfied employees have positive attitudes towards their job (Kazi & Zadeh, 2011); and absenteeism is related to job dissatisfaction (Aydogdu & Asikgil, 2011). This research did not review the attendance records of employees six months prior to the experience to the phenomena. As a result, calculations could not be made to conclude whether morale was high or low prior to the phenomena. Due to this limitation, it is difficult to ascertain; whether the recruiting and selection process caused employees to decrease morale; or if dissatisfaction due to another phenomena existed, and the current experience acted as a catalyst to decrease morale even more.

In the current research study, dissatisfaction towards the recruiting and selection processes caused employees to have a negative attitude towards their jobs and employer. As a result of a decrease in morale, dissatisfied employees thought of missing work, and or missed work for a couple of days. It is imperative that leadership understands that there exist a relationship between satisfaction and morale, such that it can cause attendance issues which can influence the morale of the department and possibly productivity. Productivity can be affected because employees have to be at work in order to produce. And if at work, a positive attitude is needed to ensure high quality in services and products, and reduce error ratios. Revamping the recruiting and selection process can increase morale, and cause employees to have a positive attitude toward their work.

Another important factor investigated in this study was Performance. The performance of employees determines how well a company does. The performance of employees is evident in the quality of services, quality of products and quantity of output. Current literature on the correlation between satisfaction and performance indicates a weak to moderate relationship between the variables. Reman and Waheed (2011) noted a moderate relationship, and Hausknecht et al. (2009) noted that when employees are dissatisfied customer dissatisfaction also decreases. Mahmood et al. (2011) asserted that the performance of an organization is affected by employee satisfaction. Leadership must recognize that the profitability of organizations in this global competitive market is contingent on the satisfaction of their employees.

As was evident in the current research study, dissatisfied employees lacked fervor to perform, and some decreased their performance. Although the performance of 41% of participants stayed the same, 50% had some evidence of a decrease in quality, quantity or both and 9% increased their performance. In an organization where 50% of employees are dissatisfied and lack fervor to perform, there is bound to be a detriment to the survival of that organization. This research did not review performance appraisals of employees six months to one year prior to experience with the phenomena. The inability to review prior performance makes it difficult to determine whether participants were high, mediocre or low performers prior to dissatisfaction with the phenomena.

Previously recorded performance would have proved useful in helping the researcher examine a marked difference between performance prior to, and after experiencing the recruiting and selection process. Prior performance appraisals would have helped in establishing whether the: 9% who increased their performance were already high performers; 41% who stayed the same were previously average performers; 50% showed a decrease were previously low performance. If there was a significant difference in previous and current performance, then it can be ascertained that dissatisfaction with the recruiting and selection process influenced performance significantly.

Leadership can empower employees who lack the skills and knowledge for promotions to attend training, so as to attain growth and development. Acquiring new skills and knowledge will help such employees to assume more responsibilities, and or to work on challenging assignments. Trevor and Nyberg (2008) posit that programs that develop the skills of employees prepare them for internal opportunities. Through promotions and the ability to work on challenging assignments, satisfaction will increase and it should influence performance.

Turnover like performance affects the profitability of business and is very costly to organizations. Literature on the correlation between turnover and performance; and turnover and satisfaction uncovered many reasons that should be helpful to leaders who want to retain their valued employees, and reduce turnover associated costs. Voluntary turnover of low performers is good (Weller et al., 2009) since such employees do not perform to increase the profitability of the organization. However, continuous voluntary turnover amongst high performers can be a detriment to the quality of service, production and organizational performance. Hausknecht et al. (2009) noted that turnover affects the services that customers receive, and Kacmar et al. (2006) indicated that turnover influences efficiency. Aydogdu and Asikgil (2011) noted that dissatisfied employees are quicker to leave their employers than satisfied employees, and Mobley (1977) concluded that dissatisfied employees are likely to leave but choose to stay because of some factors and or risks. Furthermore, Rehman and Waheed (2011) asserted that satisfied employees have commitment to the organization.

Retaining employees, especially high performers, is critical to organizational success since employees are needed to produce and provide services for customers. Investing in employees is a key to increasing organizational commitment. Leadership should show that they value their employees by: creating growth opportunities, increasing skills, and providing tools for success. As leadership, increases satisfaction, performance will increase, there will be commitment to organizational vision and intent to leave and or turnover will decrease.

The results of this qualitative research study showed that an ineffective recruiting and selection process can hamper employee satisfaction. Findings showed that there is a correlation between satisfaction to the process, and morale, because some participants' attitude was negative due to dissatisfaction with the recruiting and selection process. The wrong attitude towards their jobs and or their employer demotivated participants to go to work. When they did show up at work, they barely increased their productivity or efficiency. Instead, they lacked fervor and performed mediocre or less than par. Being dissatisfied and having low morale also propelled participants to think of leaving, but the risk associated with leaving forced many to remain within the organization.

Reducing dissatisfaction will enable organizations to get the best out of their employees; the best attitude, the best performance, more commitment, and fewer turnovers. Human Resources should create a better process for recruiting and empower decision makers in the selection process to communicate effectively, honestly and immediately. Communication throughout the process is necessary to maintain satisfaction, and it requires decision makers to inform applicants and candidates of their applications, and or candidacy. Communication should be quick and immediate after each phase, regardless of whether it is via email, phone or in-person. Human Resources' best practices should encourage the promotion of internal talent, and highlight the need for all internal applicants and internal candidates to have a good experience.

Participants in the current research study purported to the lack and delayed feedback as a catalyst that increased their dissatisfaction. Employees who are declined promotions should be informed of, and empowered to attend training programs. The training programs should increase their skills and knowledge, which will in turn help them to be more competitive for internal job openings. Providing training programs will increase the value of employees and foster commitment to the organization, increase retention, thereby reducing intent to quit and or turnover.

How can Leadership use this Study to benefit their Workforce?

The factors that were important to employees can assist Human Resources and leaders who participate in the recruiting and selection process should they consider revamping the Process. This will have a positive impact on employees and increase the performance of the organization. Employees desire security in their positions, and they want skills that will make them marketable within and outside the organization. Thus, employees want to participate in a recruiting and selection process that helps them to acquire the needed growth. They want Human Resources and the leaders involved in the selection process to provide honest and immediate feedback about their candidacy. In addition, should they fail to get promoted employees want to know why, and if it was due to a deficiency in skills and knowledge, then training is expected.

Human Resources should partner with the Training and Development team to develop programs that will provide employees with the knowledge, skills and abilities needed to acquire future promotions. A plan should be in place to refer internal applicants and internal candidates who do not progress through the recruiting process to attend training. Human Resources and other leadership should encourage employees who participated in the recruiting and selection process, but did not obtain a promotion to attend the training. The advantages of the training program should be stressed to internal applicants and internal candidates so as to increase participation in the program.

A succession plan can also be in place where Human Resources identify key positions within the organization. Human Resources and line managers identify high potentials; track their skills, abilities and past experiences. Human Resources will then select out of this talent pool and have these employees interview for the identified key positions. This plan when effective can increase the satisfaction of high performers, because it shows that leadership values them. It also shows other employees that increasing performance creates opportunities for advancement.

Human Resources can also work with other leaders to create a mentorship program where employees who were not promoted can be partnered with identified high potentials, and or successful leaders. This program will promote relationships and increase communication between the mentors and mentees. Mentors can provide advice on: on goal setting, career goals, and the knowledge, skills and abilities needed for promotions. The mentorship program can also create networking relationships within the organization for employees who did not obtain promotional growth opportunities. The mentorship program coupled with training and development programs, and or succession planning can increase employee commitment to the organization and increase retention.

Considering these factors will increase employee satisfaction. When satisfaction increases, morale will increase, because employees will have a positive attitude towards their job and leadership. With a positive attitude towards their job, employees will reduce tardiness and absenteeism. A positive attitude towards the job and employer will help employees to perform and meet deliverables. Ybema et al (2010) indicated that production decreases when employees are absent from work, because there are fewer people at work to produce. Thus, when employee attitude is positive, commitment to the organization can be enhanced. As employees begin to commit to the organization due to satisfaction and high morale, intent to leave and turnover should decrease.

What Additional Research might be Necessary?

While the research study yielded themes that revealed the commonalities in experiences to the recruiting and selection process, there are limitations that make it impossible for the study to be generalized to the general population. To ensure that the study can be generalized, future research should be conducted in various industries, using similar questions to determine if factors identified in this study as important will be the same. Other research should also examine: the relationship between morale and performance; and satisfaction, morale and high performers.

Although the findings in this study showed a direct relationship between the phenomena, satisfaction and morale, the relationship between the phenomena, morale and performance was not very clear. A significant number of participants were dissatisfied and it decreased morale, yet, with low morale, performance did not significantly decrease as expected. Permission to review attendance records and exit interviews was not granted, to identify absentee rates and the frequency of tardiness before and after promotion was denied. The ability to review such records can boost findings on the correlation between satisfaction and morale. Exit interviews can reveal the causes of voluntary turnover.

The review of performance appraisals before experience to the phenomena is necessary to identify high, mediocre, and low performers, with the aim of knowing: the satisfaction of high performers in comparison to other performers. Every organization needs high performers to help them achieve goals and profitability. Employers will benefit from knowing what influences the performance of their high performers and other potentials. If performance is high and it decreases after an experience to the phenomena, then leadership can identify the causes of the decrease in performance and work to curtail or remove it. If satisfaction is low amongst high performers, then it can be hypothesized that morale will be low, and there might be potential issues with performance and turnover. Such pertinent information will be helpful to leadership so they can work on increasing satisfaction of high performers, close the skill gap of average performers and identify the right job fit for low performers.

Using these recommendations to expand on the current research study can benefit global organizations, since employers need satisfied employees to achieve organizational goals. Expanding on this research study will provide leadership with relevant data: on factors that are important to employees; on attendance records, performance appraisals; and exit interviews to create various programs that increases satisfaction. With information from the expanded studies employers can work on increasing satisfaction as they create programs that increases performance and retention, and curtails costs associated with absenteeism and turnover.

REFERENCES

Allen, D. G., Renn, R. W., Moffitt, K. R., & Vardaman, J. M. (2007). Risky business: The role of risk in voluntary turnover decisions. *Human Resources Management Review, 17*(3), 305-318. Retrieved from http:// search.proquest.com.libproxy. edmc.edu/docview/ 884718750

Alreck, P. L. & Settle, R. B. (2004). *Survey Research Handbook* (3rd ed.). New York, NY: McGraw-Hill Irwin

Asvir, N., Ahmad, U., & Bushra, F. (2011). Promotion: A predictor of job satisfaction a study of glass house industry of Lahore (Pakistan). *International Journal of Business and Social Science, 2*(16), 1-6. Retrieved from http://search.proquest. com.libproxy.edmc.edu/ docview/904521639/

Aydogdu, S. & Asikgil, B. (2011). An Empirical Study of the Relationship among Job Satisfaction, Organizational Commitment and Turnover Intention. *International Review of Management and Marketing, 1*(3), 43-53. Retrieved from http://search. proquest.com.libproxy.edmc.edu/docview/920865004

Butcher, J., & Kritsonis, W. A. (2007). Human resource management: Managerial efficacy in recruiting and retaining teachers-- national implications. *Online Submission; the Lamar University Electronic Journal of Student Research Sum 2007,* 1-9. Retrieved from http://www. eric.ed.gov/contentdelivery/servlet/ERICServlet?accno=ED497357

Cho, S. Johanson, M. M., & Guchait, P. (2009). Employees intent to leave: A comparison of determinants of intent to leave versus intent to stay. *International Journal of Hospitality Management, 28*(3), 374-381. Retrieved from http://www. sciencedirect.com.libproxy. edmc.edu/ science/article/pii/S0278431908001023

Cho, Y. J. & Perry, J. L. (2011). Intrinsic motivation and employee attitudes: Role of managerial trustworthiness, goal directedness, and extrinsic reward expectancy. *Review of Public Personnel Administration*. Advance online publicatioFn.doi: 10.1177/0734371X11421495

Creswell, J. C. (2009). *Research Design: Qualitative, Quantitative and Mixed Methods Approaches,* (3rd ed.). Thousand Oaks, CA: Sage Publications

Creswell, J. C. (2007*). Qualitative Inquiry and Research Design: Choosing Among Five Approaches*, (2nd ed.). Thousand Oaks, CA: Sage Publications

Daft, R.L. (2008). *The leadership Experience,* (4th ed.). Mason, OH: South-Western

De Pater, I. E., Van Vianen, A. M., Bechtoldt, M. N., & Klehe, U. (2009). Employees' challenging job experiences and supervisors' evaluations of promotability. *Personnel Psychology, 62*(2), 297-325. Retrieved from http://search.proquest. com.libproxy.edmc. edu/docview/220143659/fulltextPDF?accountid=34899

Edwards, B. D., Bell, S. T., Arthur, W. Jr., & Decuir, A. D. (2008). Relationships between facets of job satisfaction and task and contextual performance. *Applied Psychology: An International Review, 57*(3), 441-465. Retrieved from http:// web. ebscohost.com.libproxy.edmc. edu/ehost/pdfviewer/pdfviewer?sid=88d7e06b-8587-4029-b70b-94c0acbd972%40 sessionmgr13&vid=2&hid=13

George, J. M., & Jones, G. R. (2008). *Understanding and Managing Organizational Behavior,* (5th ed.). Upper Saddle River, NJ: Pearson Prentice Hall

Goldsmith, M., Greenberg, C., Alastair, R., & Hu-Chan, M. (2003). *Global Leadership: The Next Generation for Education Management Corporation.* Upper Saddle River, NJ: Financial Times Prentice Hall

Gill, A., Sharma, S. P., Mathur, N., & Bhutani, S. (2012). The effects of job satisfaction and work experience on employee-desire for empowerment: A comparative study in Canada and India. *International Journal of Management, 29*(1), 190-200. Retrieved from http://search.proquest. com.libproxy.edmc.edu/docview/925800805/fulltextPDF

Harman, W. S., Lee, T. W., Mitchell, T. R., Felps, W., & Owens, B. P. (2007). The psychology of voluntary employee turnover. *Current Directions in Psychological Science, 16(*1), 51-54. Retrieved from http:// web.ebscohost.com.libproxy.

edmc.edu/ehost/pdfviewer/pdfvie wer?sid=d2dd95ec-fdb7-4a54-ba43-99d 6b517 e416%40sessionmgr111&vid=2&hid=110

Harris, A., & Guillemin, M. (2012). Developing sensory awareness in qualitative interviewing: A portal into the otherwise unexplored. *Qualitative Health Research, 22*(5), 689-701. Retrieved from http://qhr.sagepub.com.libproxy.edmc.edu/content/22/5/689

Hausknecht, J. P., Trevor, C. O., & Howard, M. J. (2009). Unit –level voluntary turnover rates and customer service quality: Implications of group cohesiveness, newcomer concentration and size. *Journal of Applied Psychology, 94*(4), 1068-1075. Retrieved fromhttp://search.proquest.com.libproxy.edmc.edu/ docview/14509832

Herzberg, F. (2003). One more time: How do you motivate employees? *Harvard Business Review, 81*(1), 87-96. Retrieved from http://web.ebscohost.com.

Lib proxy.edmc.edu/ehost/pdfviewer/pdfviewer?sid=e930b689

Hom, P. W., Roberson, L., & Ellis, A. D. (2008). Challenging conventional wisdom about who quits: Revelations from corporate America. *Journal of Applied Psychology, 93*(1), 1-34. Retrieved from http://search.proquest.com.libproxy.edmc.edu/docview/614499069

Hsiung, P. (2008). Teaching reflexivity in qualitative interviewing. *Teaching Sociology, 36*(3), 211-226. Retrieved from http://search.proquest.com.libproxy.edmc.edu/ docview/ 223522032/fulltextPDF?accountid=34899

Huning, T. M., & Thomson, N. F. (2011). An empirical examination of the impact of performance attributions and job satisfaction on turnover intentions. *Journal of Organizational Culture, Communication and Conflict, 15*(1), 121-130. Retrieved from http://search.proquest.com.libproxy.edmc.edu/docview/886553287

Kacmar, K. M., Andrews, M. C., Van Rooy, D. L., Steilberg, R. C., & Cerrone, S. (2006). Sure everyone can be replaced but at what cost? Turnover as a predictor of unit-level performance. *Academy of Management Journal, 49*(1), 133-144. Retrieved fromhttp://search.proquest.com.libproxy.edmc.edu/docview/199793509

Kazi, G. M., & Zadeh, Z. F. (2011). The Contribution of Individual Variables: Job Satisfaction and Job Turnover. *Interdisciplinary Journal of Contemporary Research in Business, 3* (5), 984-991. Retrieved from http://search.proquest.com. libproxy.edmc.edu/docview/904424079/ fulltextPDF?accountid=34899

Kouzes, J. M., & Posner, B. Z. (2007). *The Leadership Challenge,* (4th ed.). San Francisco, CA: Jossey-Bass

Kuzmits, F., Adams, A. (2009). Improving Employee Attendance with No-fault Absenteeism. *The Business Review, Cambridge, 14*(1), 280-285. Retrieved from http://search.proquest. com.edmc.edu/ docview/197304575/fulltextPDF?accounted=34899

Labuschagne, A. (2003). Qualitative research – airy fairy or fundamental? *The qualitative Report, 8*(1), 100-103. Retrieved from http://www. nova.edu/ssss/QR/QR8-1/ labuschagne.pdf

Laurent, W. (2008). Human resources and recruiting management. *Information Management, 18*(6), 15. Retrieved from http://search. proquest.com/docview/ 214669761?accountid =34899

Lee, T. H., Gerhart, B., Weller, I. & Trevor, C.O. (2008). Understanding voluntary turnover: Path-specific job satisfaction effects and the importance of unsolicited job offers. *Academy of Management Journal, 51*(4), 651-671. Retrieved from http://search.proq uest.com.libproxy.edmc.edu/docview/199788734   /abstract? source=fedsrch&accountid=34899

Lloyd, J. (2012, February1). How to manage an employee's roller-coaster performance. *The Receivables Report, 27*(2), 9-10. Retrieved from http://search.proquest.com. libproxy.edmc.edu/ docview/915869361/ fulltextPDF?accountid=34899

Macfarlane, I. (2008, February 1). Finding a qualified employee starts with hiring process. *Wisconsin State Journal,* pp. 9. Retrieved from http:// search.proquest. com/docview/391507873?accountid=34899

Mahmood, S., Mirza, W. A., Khan, B. A., & Talib, N. (2011). The legacy job satisfaction and its impact on performance of the firm: and empirical analysis. *Interdisciplinary Journal of Contemporary Research in Business, 3*(2), 790-803. Retrieved from http://search.proquest.com.libproxy. edmc.edu/docview/878741 565 /fulltextPDF?accountid=34899

Maxwell, J.A. (1992). Understanding and validity in qualitative research. *Harvard Educational Review, 62*(3), 279-300. Retrieved from http://

search.proquest.com. libproxy.edmc. edu/docview/212250067/fulltextPDF?accountid=34899

McGuigan, P. J., & Stamatelos, L. J. (2011). The ten commandments of recruiting: Best practices for hiring the best employees. *The Journal of Medical Practice Management, 26*(5), 296-298. Retrieved from http://search.proquest.com. libproxy.edmc.edu/docview/910698976

Miles, M. B., & Huberman, M. (1984). Drawing valid meaning from qualitative data: Toward a shared craft. *Educational Researcher, 13*(5), 20-30. Retrieved from http://edr.sagepub. com.libproxy.edmc.edu/content/13/5/20.full.pdf+html

Mobley, W. H. (1977). Intermediate linkages in the relationship between job satisfaction and employee turnover. *Journal of Applied Psychology 62*(2), 237-240. Retrieved from http://search.proquest.com.libproxy.edmc.edu/ docview/ 614356238/fulltext PDF

Morgan, G., Smircich, L. (1980). The case for qualitative research. *Academy of Management, 5*(4), 491-500. Retrieved from http://search.proquest.com.libproxy. edmc edu/docview/230059070/fulltextPDF?accountid=34899

Moustakas, C. (1994). *Phenomenological research methods.* Thousand Oaks, CA: Sage Publications

Mukherjee, W. (2011, January 19). Five ways to pump up employee morale. *The Economic Times.* Retrieved from http://search.proquest.com. libproxy.edmc.edu/ docview/851939123

Murray, L. M., & Fischer, A. K. (2010). Strategic recruiting: A human resource management case study. *Journal of Business Case Studies, 6*(6), 97-102. Retrieved from http://search.proquest.com/docview/818381297?accountid=34899

Nyberg, A. (2010). Retaining your high performers: Moderators of the performance-job satisfaction-voluntary turnover relationship. *Journal of Applied Psychology, 95*(3), 440-453. Retrieved from http://search.proquest.com.libproxy.edmc. edu/docview/614520278

Office of Federal Contract Compliance Programs (2010). What is an applicant? Retrieved from http://www.ofccp.com/what_is_an_applicant.htm

Pare, G. & Tremblay, M. (2006). The influence of high involvement human resources practices, procedural justice, organizational commitment, and citizenship behaviors on information technology professionals' turnover intentions. *Group & Organizational Management, 32*(3), 326-357. Retrieved from http://search.proquest.com.libproxy.edmc.edu/docview/ 203362660

Pearce, C. (2007). Ten steps to conducting a selection interview. *Nursing Management, 14*(5), 21-21. http://search.proquest.com/docview/236916623?accountid=34899

Perkins, J. (2011). Hiring 2.0: 23 Creative Ways to Recruit and Keep Great Staff. *Public Management, 93*(1), 16. Retrieved from http://elibrary.bigchalk.com
.libproxy.edmc.

Podsakoff, N. P., LePine, J. A., & LePine, M. A. (2007). Differential challenge stressor-hindrance stressor relationships with job attitudes, turnover intentions, turnover, and withdrawal behavior: A meta-analysis. *American Psychology Association, 92*(2), 438-454. Retrieved from http://search.proquest.com.libproxy.edmc. edu/docview/614465613

Preenen, P. T. Y., De Pater, I. E., Van Vianen, A. E. M., Keijzer, L. (2011). Managing voluntary turnover through challenging assignments. Group & Organization Management, 36(3), 308-344. Retrieved from http://gom.sagepub.com.libproxy. edmc.edu/content/36/3/308

Rehman, M. S., & Waheed, A. (2011). An empirical study of impact of job satisfaction on job performance in the public sector organizations. *Interdisciplinary Journal of Contemporary Research in Business, 2*(9), 167-181. Retrieved from http://search. proquest.com.libproxy.edmc. edu/docview/857735040/fulltextPDF?accountid=34899

Schoenherr, J. A. (2009, February 27). The Three R's. *Chronicle of Higher Education.* Retrieved from http://chronicle.com.libproxy.edmc.edu/article/The-Three-Rs/44866/

Singer, P., & Goodrich, J. (2006). Retaining and motivating high-performing employees. *Public Libraries, 45*(1), 58-63. Retrieved from http://search.proquest.com/docview/ 217457167?accountid=34899

Shaikh, M. A. Bhutto, N. M. & Maitlo, Q. (2012). Facets of job satisfaction and its association with performance. International Journal of Business and Social Science, *3*(7), 322-326. Retrieved from http://search.proquest.com.libproxy. edmc.edu/docview/1010400542

Swider, B. W., Boswell, W. R., & Zimmerman, R. D. (2011). Examining the job search-turnover relationship: The role of embeddedness, job satisfaction, and available alternatives. *Journal of Applied Psychology, 96*(2), 432-441. Retrieved from http://search.proquest.com.libproxy. edmc.edu/docview/849639870/ fulltextPDF?accountid=34899

Tracey, J. B. & Hinkin, T. R. (2008). Contextual factors and cost profiles associated with employee turnover. *Cornell Hospital Quarterly, 49*(1), 12-27. Retrieved from http://cqx.sagepub.com.libproxy.edmc.edu/content/49/1/12.full.pdf+html

Trevor, C. O., Nyberg, A. J (2008). Keeping your headcount when about you are losing theirs: Downsizing, voluntary turnover rates, and the moderating role of HR practices. *Academy of Management Journal, 51*(2), 259-276. Retrieved from http://search.proquest.com.lib proxy.edmc.edu/docview/199783303

Tuzun, I. K. (2007). Antecedents of turnover intention toward a service provider. *The Business Review, 8*(2), 128-134. Retrieved from http://search.proquest.com.libproxy.edmc.edu/docview/197306510/ fulltextPDF? accountid=34899

Ullah, M. M. (2010). A systematic approach of conducting employee selection interview. *International Journal of Business and Management, 5*(6), 106-112. Retrieved from http://search.proquest.com/docview/821544594?accountid=34899

Van Manen, M. (2006). Writing qualitatively, or the demands of writing. *Qualitative Health Research, 16*(5), 713-722. Retrieved from http://qhr.sagepub.com. libproxy.edmc.edu/ content/16/5/713.full.pdf+html

Watt, D. (2007). On becoming a qualitative researcher: The value of reflexivity. *The Qualitative Report, 12*(1), 82-101. Retrieved from http://www.eric.ed.gov/ PDFS/EJ800164.pdf

Weller, I., Holtom, B. C., Matiaske, W., & Mellewigt, T. (2009). Level and time effects of recruitment sources on early voluntary turnover. *American Psychological Association, 94*(5), 1146-1162. Retrieved from http://search.proquest.com. libproxy.edmc.edu/doc view/ 614503920/ fulltextPDF?accountid=34899

Westover, J. H., Westover, A. R., & Westover, L. A. (2010). Enhancing long-term worker productivity and performance. The connection of key work domains to job satisfaction and organizational commitment. *International Journal of Productivity and Performance Management, 59*(4), 372-387. Retrieved from http://search.proquest.com.libproxy. edmc. edu/docview/218426873/ fulltextPDF?accountid=34899

White, G. L. (1995). Employee turnover: The hidden drain on profits. *HR Focus, 72*(1), 15-18. Retrieved from http://search.proquest.com. libproxy.edmc.edu/docview/ 206785986

Yang, J., Wan, C., & Fu, Y. (2012). Qualitative examination of employee turnover and retention strategies in international tourist hotels in Taiwan. *International Journal of Hospitality Management, 31*(3), 837-848. Retrieved from http://www.science direct.com.libproxy.edmc. edu/science/article/pii/S0278431911001642

Ybema, J. F., Smulders, P. G. W., & Bongers, P. M. (2010). Antecedents and consequences of employee absenteeism: A longitudinal perspective on the role of job satisfaction and burnout. *European Journal of Work and Organizational Psychology, 19* (1), 102-124. Retrieved from http:// www.tandfonline.com. libproxy.edmc.edu/doi/abs/10.1080/13594 320902793691

Zimmerman, R. D., & Darnold, T.C. (2007). The impact of job performance on employee turnover intentions and the voluntary turnover process. *Personnel Review 38* (2), 142-148. Retrieved from http://search.proquest.com.libproxy.edmc.edu/docview/21480531 5/ fulltextPDF?accountid=34899

APPENDIX A

Interview Questions

1. Discuss your satisfaction after you went through the recruiting and selection process for a promotional opportunity?
2. Discuss how you felt after you went through the recruiting and selection process?
3. How did the experience affect your desire to go to work every day of the week?
4. Discuss how your production and efficiency was affected after you experienced the recruiting and selection process?
5. Discuss how you felt about your employment after you went through the recruiting and selection process

Printed in the United States
By Bookmasters